Clear and to the Point

Clear and to the Point

8 Psychological Principles for Compelling PowerPoint Presentations

Stephen M. Kosslyn

OXFORD
UNIVERSITY PRESS

2007

OXFORD
UNIVERSITY PRESS

Oxford University Press, Inc., publishes works that further
Oxford University's objective of excellence
in research, scholarship, and education.

Oxford New York
Auckland Cape Town Dar es Salaam Hong Kong Karachi
Kuala Lumpur Madrid Melbourne Mexico City Nairobi
New Delhi Shanghai Taipei Toronto

With offices in
Argentina Austria Brazil Chile Czech Republic France Greece
Guatemala Hungary Italy Japan Poland Portugal Singapore
South Korea Switzerland Thailand Turkey Ukraine Vietnam

Published by Oxford University Press, Inc.
198 Madison Avenue, New York, New York 10016

www.oup.com

Oxford is a registered trademark of Oxford University Press

Library of Congress Cataloging-in-Publication Data
Kosslyn, Stephen Michael, 1948–
Clear and to the point:
8 psychological principles for compelling
powerpoint presentations / Stephen M. Kosslyn.
p. cm.
Includes index.
ISBN 978-0-19-532069-5 (pbk.)
1. Presentation graphics software.
2. Microsoft PowerPoint (Computer file) I. Title.
P93.53.M534K67 2007
006.6'869—dc22   2006100013

5 7 9 8 6

Printed in the United States of America
on acid-free paper

To my wife, Robin

Contents

Preface

The PowerPoint program is like the weather: Everybody likes to complain about it, but nobody does anything about it. This book is an attempt to clear the PowerPoint skies. With the PowerPoint program, people complain the most about the presentations it allows users to produce, which can be irritating, confusing, boring, condescending, and incomprehensible. I doubt that creators of those presentations intend to come off in any of these ways, but they simply haven't had guidance in how to use this medium to be *clear and to the point.* This book's mission is to provide that guidance.

The happy confluence of two activities led to this book. First, I revised my earlier book, *Elements of Graph Design*, so thoroughly that it was re-named *Graph Design for the Eye and Mind.* While working on that project, I noticed that the same psychological principles extend beyond graph design to all visual communication. Those principles of perception and cognition are at work no matter what we humans are doing, be it interpreting graphs, playing golf, reading tea leaves, or anything else (including giving PowerPoint presentations). Second, I was a member of many search committees in my department, which involved sitting through innumerable PowerPoint presentations that—ironically (given that I'm in a department of psychology)—violated psychological principles.

Unlike other books I've written on communication graphics, this one isn't an academic discussion. (That should be obvious by the time you get to the joke about vampire bats.) I've given you only what you can use right now. (If you want to know about the scientific studies that back up my principles and recommendations, look at the detailed discussions of the relevant empirical literature and the long list of references in *Graph Design for the Eye and Mind.*)

I have many people to thank for inspiring and helping me make this book a reality. Catharine Carlin of the Oxford University Press came through once again (this is my third book with her). Her time, trouble, and good sense were extremely valued at every step along the way. Also at Oxford, Lelia Mander did a superb job in managing the production of this book, and I again thank her for her clear-headed, good judgment. My agent, Rafe Sagalyn, not only read the manuscript and made extraordinarily constructive suggestions, but he also broke the logjam over the title (and came up with the one that graces the cover). Rafe is everything an agent should be and much more. I also thank my assistant, Alex Russell, for lending me her sharp eye, and my student Sam Moulton, PowerPoint maven supreme, for going over the manuscript in detail and sparing no words in setting me straight. (Any remaining errors are not his fault, but rather reflect my own foibles.) Andrew Shultman and Patricia Leigh Zadnik also helped make the earliest drafts begin to approach coherence. And Nicholas C. Liu helped put the manuscript together, with patience and good humor, Jennifer Shephard helped in too many ways to enumerate, and Stefano Imbert and David Kosslyn provided invaluable image design ideas and produced some of the most interesting illustrations in the book. Ronnie Lipton gave the manuscript an extraordinarily close read, and made invaluable suggestions (as well as uncounted specific edits). Thanks, Ronnie! Finally, I must thank my family: Robin—for giving me the space to do this project, in spite of looming deadlines on our jointly authored textbooks—and our children, Justin, David, and Neil—all of whom contributed valuable insights and observations.

Clear and to the Point

Introduction to Articulate Presentations

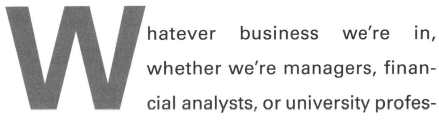hatever business we're in, whether we're managers, financial analysts, or university professors, we are very likely to suffer through frequent PowerPoint presentations. We see them everywhere—not only at meetings but also online. If we stop to think about it, most of these presentations are dreadfully put together, and either they confuse us or attempt to lull us into accepting weak arguments uncritically. PowerPoint presentations are now parodied, disparaged, and blamed for failures to communicate clearly.

As a professor of psychology who has written widely about how humans process information, some years ago I found myself paying as much attention to the medium as to the message. I began keeping a log of the problems in PowerPoint presentations I saw, and I realized that virtually all of them occur because the presentations failed to respect fundamental characteristics of how we humans perceive, remember, and comprehend information.

I decided to write this book to make the relevant psychological principles clear to people who didn't study these fundamental characteristics of the human mind, and to show how anyone can use these principles to make crystal clear, compelling presentations. This book is fundamentally different from all other books on creating PowerPoint presentations. My recommendations not only are firmly rooted in well-known psychological principles, but I also show you, the reader, how to use these principles to create presentations that communicate clearly and effectively—that are clear and to the point.

When I speak of "psychological principles," I'm not referring to our understanding of neurotic tendencies or any of the things Freud might have discussed during his sessions with patients on the couch. Rather, I am referring to the fruits of the modern science of psychology, which aims in part to discover how perception, memory, comprehension, cognition, motivation, and emotion operate. With the advent of cognitive psychology (which seeks to understand such mental processes by analogy to the operation of computer programs) in the second half of the 20th century and the more recent emergence of cognitive neuroscience (which aims to discover how the brain gives rise to mental processes), we now know more than enough to apply our knowledge to the design of multimedia presentations.

The recommendations offered in this book will help you to make and deliver an effective presentation, step by step—but don't think I'm going to tie you down with rules that will make your presentation formulaic, dry, or lacking in personal style. Your creativity will have plenty of leeway. At the same time, if you design your presentation according to the recommendations I offer here, you will play to the strengths of those who see and hear it, and will avoid being defeated—that is, misunderstood or ignored—because of the inherent weaknesses of human mental processes.

The aims of this book rest on the idea that there's nothing fundamentally wrong with the PowerPoint program as a medium; rather, I claim that the problem lies in how it is used. This view is not universally shared, and you might wonder whether I can deliver on my promises. For example, Edward Tufte, the modern guru of visual communication, claims that the PowerPoint program is inherently flawed. He has found the problems with this tool so pervasive and destructive that he challenges the very idea of using it to communicate.

Before accepting Tufte's verdict, however, consider an analogy: Both an assault rifle and a hammer can be used to kill, but the assault rifle *invites* mayhem, whereas this is an incidental application of a hammer. With regard to its capacity for ruining a presentation, is the PowerPoint program more like the rifle or the hammer? Unlike Tufte, I don't see it as akin to the weapon, which invites being used in the service of destruction. The PowerPoint program is much more like a hammer. Or, more accurately, it's more like a word processing program than an assault rifle. Just as you wouldn't blame Microsoft Word for every bad article you've read, you shouldn't blame the PowerPoint program for every bad presentation you've seen.

In fact, this medium is a remarkably versatile tool that can be extraordinarily effective. Rather than the program's being fundamentally flawed, the problem is that some users, like kids in a candy store, become gluttonous consumers of the options presented by the PowerPoint program—and forget to focus on nutrition. We should use these presentations not to razzle-dazzle with eye candy but to give the meat of our ideas. In this book I provide clear instructions that you can follow to make your ideas crystal clear and immediately comprehensible. But I also go deeper than that—I aim to help you develop intuitions about how to use this powerful tool effectively.

Three Goals and How to Achieve Them

The advice I offer in this book will help you build and deliver presentations that accomplish three goals that virtually define an effective presentation:

Goal 1: *Connect with your audience.*
　Your message should connect with the goals and interests of your audience.
Goal 2: *Direct and hold attention.*
　You should lead the audience to pay attention to what's important.
Goal 3: *Promote understanding and memory.*
　Your presentation should be easy to follow, digest, and remember.

These obviously are worthy goals. The trick is how to achieve them—and that's what this book is about. You can achieve each of these goals if you respect the eight psychological principles that I summarize beneath their applicable goals (and describe in detail in the Appendix). These principles will in turn lead to very specific recommendations in the chapters that follow.

In this introductory chapter, my aim is to give you an overview and a general sense of the eight principles that underlie my advice. We now consider the three goals. When turning to each goal, I introduce the principles that will help to accomplish it.

Goal 1: Connect with Your Audience

You'll communicate effectively only when you focus the audience's attention and interest on a specific message. When I first began to speak publicly, I thought that the goal was to convey as much information on a topic as possible and utterly failed to connect with the audience; I would present many summaries and examples and swamp the audience, not knowing what was of interest to them. I was giving talks to myself, not to the members of the audience (which was doubly unfortunate, since I already knew what I had to say!). You need to speak *to* your audience, not speak *at* them.

Two principles will help you achieve this goal.

Principle 1. The Principle of Relevance
Communication is most effective when neither too much nor too little information is presented.

Abraham Lincoln was once asked how long a man's legs should be. His answer: Long enough to reach the ground. A talk is like a man's legs: It should be as long, but no longer, than necessary to get the job done—in this case, to convey your message. I've never once heard somebody complain that a presentation was too short.

This principle has two main aspects:

1. A presentation must be built from the outset around your take-home message; every aspect of the presentation should be relevant to what you want the audience to know and believe when they walk out the door. We don't want to put ourselves in the position of Yogi Berra when he declared "I didn't really say everything I said."
2. The audience should be told only what they must know to get your message: Telling them too little will leave them puzzled—and telling them too much will leave them overwhelmed, disoriented, and irritated (and ultimately bored, because they will stop trying to track what you are saying). Telling people too much is like what used to happen when digital watches first appeared on the scene: When asked the time, people sometimes—unhelpfully and annoyingly—reported it down to the second. This was neither informative nor humorous.

Example: If you are talking about a *general* difference between Japanese and U.S. consumers, don't break the information down by gender or region.

Principle 2. The Principle of Appropriate Knowledge
Communication requires prior knowledge of pertinent concepts, jargon, and symbols.

You've no doubt often heard that you should "know your audience," and this advice is rock solid: To communicate effectively, your presentation must be pitched at the right level for the audience you wish to reach. The Principle of Relevance is about *what* to communicate, whereas the Principle of Appropriate Knowledge is about *how* to convey that information. Consider these two quotes:

He has never been known to use a word that might send a reader to the dictionary.
> — *William Faulkner (about Ernest Hemingway)*

Poor Faulkner. Does he really think big emotions come from big words?
> — *Ernest Hemingway (about William Faulkner)*

Hemingway was right in more ways than he may have realized: If a reader is sent to the dictionary, she might just as soon put down the book and walk away. To reach your audience, you need to pitch your talk at a level that makes contact with what the audience already knows. This is true in terms of three factors:

1. The *language* you use—not only the jargon you choose, but also the sophistication and complexity of both the vocabulary and syntactic structure.
2. The types of *displays* you use. For example, a standard bar graph is familiar to (almost) everyone, but a box-and-whisker chart (which typically shows the median, the range of values in the quartile above and below it, and the extreme values) is not universally understood; in fact, you—along with most people—have probably never even heard of it. If you don't recognize the format, you can empathize with how a member of the audience would feel if you violated the Principle of Appropriate Knowledge.
3. The specific *concepts* and information you draw upon. For example, everyone understands amount, but not everyone knows what a first or second derivative is.

If you assume that the members of the audience know more than they actually do and you use unfamiliar language, displays, or concepts, you will not connect with them—and actually might intimidate them. If you assume that they know less than they actually do, you'll bore them. In either case, you'll fail to connect; even if out of politeness they do manage to keep their eyes propped open and feign not falling asleep.

In short, you have three options: Go over the heads of the audience members and be perceived as a high-falutin' person who likes to hear himself or herself talk; talk down to the audience, and be taken as a patronizing boor; or think about the audience in advance and pitch your talk appropriately. The choice is clear.

In addition, you need to know your audience because your talk should address *their concerns and interests*. It's a curious fact of memory that the more we reflect on material, the more likely it is that the material will stick, that we will remember it, whether or not we've tried to do so. If you can interest your audience and engage them with the material, they will end up remembering it automatically because they will have thought about it.

> **Example:** If you are talking about the economics of oil production to your local Kiwanis group, link the abstract ideas to facets of everyday life, such as the prices of gas, fresh produce, and even various types of synthetic clothing.

Goal 2: Direct and Hold Attention

In the bad old days, before the PowerPoint program existed, speakers often would distribute handouts at the beginning of a presentation. The members of the audience then did exactly what you would expect them to do: They began to read the handout, ignoring what the speaker was saying. Adding insult to injury, they would also rustle the pages as they read, which distracted anyone who was trying to follow the presentation itself.

The modern equivalent of passing out handouts occurs when you give the viewers options about what to pay attention to on a slide. Instead of listening to you, the audience will ignore you while busily examining the slide, reading the text, and looking at the pictures. Because a presentation marches on over time, it is not like a book or paper, where the reader can set his or her own pace and go back when desired. You need to present material in a way that leads the audience through it step by step, and that does not result in their getting lost, confused, or overwhelmed.

In order for your PowerPoint presentation to communicate effectively, it must hold your audience's attention effectively. The audience should be like a boat pushed by an outboard motor, with you supplying the gas! Your talk should *not* leave the audience like so many logs drifting in the current. By using the three psychological principles noted below, in combination with the two just described, the audience will automatically pay attention to you and your message—simply because that's the path of least resistance.

Principle 3: The Principle of Salience

Attention is drawn to large perceptible differences.

Our brains are "difference detectors." We cannot help being drawn to large differences in perceptible qualities—be they the sudden movement of a rabbit in tall grass, a bright or bold pattern (**like this one**) on a dim background, or loud noises in the kitchen. Salient stimuli are those that are clearly different from the surrounding stimuli, and salient stimuli hijack the audience's attention.

> **Example:** To make the title of a slide the most salient, make it **larger and bolder** than the other text. Similarly, to highlight the most important bar in a graph, color it brighter than the others.

The Principle of Salience is important in part because of what it leads us not to do: Namely, irrelevancies should not be salient.

> **Example:** The PowerPoint program includes many infelicitous background patterns, which at first glance may be tempting eye candy. Some have conspicuous background patterns, such as beach balls and other large, multicolored objects, that grab the viewers' attention. But you don't want the audience to be lost in admiration of the background of your slides. You also don't want the audience to struggle to get your message amid gripping irrelevancies. Instead, the most important part of a slide should command their immediate attention.

This principle also leads us to prioritize different aspects of the message, highlighting what is most important at any given moment in time. Imagine that you are guiding a blindfolded person along a route by giving verbal directions: At the outset, you need to give the person an overall description of the lay of the land ("we'll be going half a mile, with about a dozen turns"), and then only tell her at the relevant times what she needs to know to complete each leg of the journey. Your audience isn't blindfolded, but needs similar guidance.

> **Example:** With the PowerPoint program, you can call attention to text or pictures by sending them in from the side; conversely, you can remove objects from the viewer's attention by making them only a shade or two different from the background color—a process that I will call "graying it out."

Principle 4: The Principle of Discriminability

Two properties must differ by a large enough proportion or they will not be distinguished.

Salience is crucial for directing and holding attention, but a change doesn't even have a chance of being paid attention to if it's not discriminable. Discriminability occurs when we can tell two things apart, whereas salience occurs when differences are so large that attention is involuntarily grabbed by the stand-out object or event. A difference of two inches in height between two toddlers is easy to notice (and hence such a difference is salient), but is essentially invisible (and hence not discriminable) when we compare two pro basketball players who are more than seven feet tall. Our visual systems register relative proportions, not absolute amounts, so that if a proportion is too small, we won't be able to distinguish between two properties. If a change is not discriminable, it may as well not be there.

> **Example.** We've all had the experience of squinting from the back of the room, trying to read a tiny label: The words are too small for us to distinguish the individual letters. Similarly, consider again those fancy and elaborate backgrounds that the PowerPoint program so conveniently provides, which range from cosmic scenes to complex geometric patterns. These backgrounds can make reading text the visual equivalent of sorting wheat from chaff, and can turn your slide into a puzzle to be solved. Even if you assume that they will bother, why make your audience work so hard?

Principle 5: The Principle of Perceptual Organization

People automatically group elements into units, which they then attend to and remember.

You can direct your audience's attention in part by how you arrange the material on your slide; viewers will consider together material that is organized into a single group. We see groups formed from individual elements all of the time. For instance, we see a flock of geese heading south for the winter not as individual birds, but instead as a unit; we see reflectors on the highway not as single pieces of plastic, but instead as a line. The same principles that lead us to organize geese or reflectors are also at work when we hear a presentation and see slides. We automatically group together:

- Objects that are near each other: We see XXX   XXX as two groups of 3 Xs, whereas we see XX   XX   XX—the same number of X marks, differently arranged—as three groups of 2 Xs.
- Objects that appear to be similar: We see XXXOOO as two groups.
- Objects that line up on a smooth curve. We see − − − − − −as a single line, but − − − _ _ _ as two lines (each of which is a group).

- Objects that move similarly: We see two words flying in from the left side of the display as grouped together.
- Objects that form simple shapes. We see [_] as a single group, but not _] [

> **Example:** Labels should be closer to the object (or, in a graph, to the wedge, line, or bar) that they label than to anything else.

Goal 3: Promote Understanding and Memory

If you take advantage of how mental processes operate, you can help the audience easily understand and retain material. Conversely, if you ignore key facts about these processes and their limitations, you will easily confuse or overwhelm the processes. The following three principles will help you promote understanding and retention (when combined with the five summarized earlier).

Principle 6: The Principle of Compatibility
A message is easiest to understand if its form is compatible with its meaning.

Our mental processes tend to make a direct connection between the properties of what we see and hear, and the content of the message being conveyed. In other words, we infer content from form. The admonition not to judge a book by its cover is necessary precisely because we have this tendency.

> **Example**. A vivid illustration of this principle was provided by John Ridley Stroop in 1935. Stroop showed people the names of colors written in various colors of ink. For example, the word "red" was written in red, blue, or green ink; the word "blue" in red, blue, or green ink, and so on. When participants were asked to report the color of the ink (not to read the word), they took more time and made more errors when the word named a color *different* from the color of the ink than when the word named a color the *same* as the color of the ink. Similar interference occurs when people are asked to judge the relative sizes of the words large and small written in small and large typefaces, respectively. We are confused when the two messages—from the form itself and from the meaning—conflict.

A particularly important aspect of this principle is our unconscious and automatic tendency to follow the dictum that *More is More.* This tendency is very clear in graphs, where an additional amount of a wedge or a bar is seen to represent an additional quantity, and a continuous rise and fall of a line is naturally taken to reflect a continuous rise and fall in the entity being measured.

Example. I once saw an egregious violation of the dictum that More is More: The artist presented a bar graph to convey the burglary rates of different cities. Each horizontal bar was made up of little pictures of houses, and longer bars represented larger numbers of houses. So far, so good. But here is the problem: Each bar, regardless of length, showed only one burglarized house (in red)—which meant that the *longer* the bar, the *lower* the rate (because the one burglarized house was a smaller percentage of the whole bar). At first glance, the reader saw the longer bars as indicating more burglaries (which was, after all, the subject of the graph) and had to fight the intuition that *more is more* to realize that longer bars actually meant "fewer." The graph would have been more effective if longer bars had simply indicated a greater percentage of burglaries.

Principle 7: The Principle of Informative Changes
People expect changes in properties to carry information.

This principle has two aspects:

1. When we see or hear a change, we expect it to mean something, so every visible or auditory change should convey information. This idea runs counter to the habits of many PowerPoint users, who include decorations or interesting (but essentially random) visual changes, thinking it makes the talk more attractive. But if words, shapes, or effects don't convey information, they distract.

   Example: Telling a joke in the middle of a presentation can give the audience time to "come up for air" (which is a good idea when the presentation is complex). But the joke must be related to the topic of the presentation. For instance, let's say I tell the following joke now (adapted from one found at www.coolfunnyjokes.com/Funny-Jokes/Animal-Jokes/ Vampire-bat.html): A vampire bat, covered in fresh blood, parked himself on the roof of the cave to get some sleep. Pretty soon all the other bats smelled the blood and began hassling him about where he got it. He told them to go away and let him get some sleep, but they persisted until finally he gave in. "OK, follow me" he said and flew out of the cave with hundreds of bats behind him. Down through the valley they swept, across a river and into a forest full of trees. Finally he slowed down and all the other bats excitedly milled around him. "Now, do you see that tree over there?" he asked. "Yes, Yes, Yes!" the bats all screamed in a frenzy. "Good," said the bat, "because I sure as hell didn't!"

Whatever its merits as humor, this joke makes no sense in the current context. If I had presented it in the discussion of discriminability, it could have helped to make the point (sort of). Or I could have used it to illustrate a violation of the Principle of Relevance. But here, it just plain doesn't fit.

This leads to the second aspect of the Principle of Informative Changes:

2. Every change in meaning should be conveyed by a change in appearance. What they see (and hear) is what they get; and what you want them to get should be signaled by something you show (or say).

Example: If part of a graph is a projection to the future, it should look different (perhaps darker or over a colored screen) from the part that summarizes actual data.

Principle 8: The Principle of Capacity Limitations

People have a limited capacity to retain and to process information, and so will not understand a message if too much information must be retained or processed.

We can hold only so much in mind and perform so many mental operations before we reach our limits. You've no doubt had the experience of over-taxing your computer, for example, by trying to download an enormous file. But unlike the tireless, steady machine, we humans are not so patient, and usually will simply give up trying if we must work too hard to decode a message or understand a presentation.

This principle has two parts:

1. We like to joke about our memory foibles (e.g., "A clear conscience is usually the sign of a bad memory"), but the truth is that people can retain only a limited amount as they try to soak in new information. In fact, the audience cannot hold in mind more than four groups of information at once—which I call the *Rule of Four*. But each group itself can contain four groups.

Example: Showing all 64 boxes in a complex organizational chart will overwhelm the audience. But the audience can absorb this information if you build up the slide a portion at a time. For instance, you can present the top layers (where proximity will group them first), and then show successive lower layers on the slide (graying out the upper layers, to direct attention to the new material—but keeping the grayed-out portions just barely discriminable in order to preserve the overall context). Or, you could use color to define the different perceptual groups, each of which should contain no more than four entities.

2. Effort is required to search for information or mentally transform information. Abraham Lincoln was not being complimentary when he said of an acquaintance, "He can compress the most words into the smallest idea of any man I know." An audience should not have to search through a visual or conceptual haystack to find the needle you are talking about.

Example: I once gave a talk in which I argued that it's worthwhile to study a very difficult, perhaps ultimately intractable, scientific problem (understanding the nature of human motivation). In this talk, I used a variant of Pascal's Wager, which is an argument for believing in God. Pascal essentially set up a 2 × 2 table: The two columns were labeled "God Doesn't Exist" and "God Exists," and the rows were labeled "You Believe in God" and "You Don't Believe in God." I described these columns and rows aloud, and then worked through the four cells, pointing out the crucial cell, which combines "You Don't Believe" and "God Exists." So, the argument goes, given the major downside of being in this cell, and the very small downsides (if any) of the other three cells in the table, you may as well believe. I would then apply this argument to studying my Hard Problem, saying that if it's possible to understand it, we'll lose big-time if we don't try.

However, it turned out that the real "Hard Problem" for the audience was mentally transforming my words into a visual mental image of the 2 × 2 table, keeping the labels straight in their heads, and then mentally scanning from cell to cell. I often lost the audience, and failed to convert them to my point of view. I solved this problem by actually showing a table (with abbreviated labels), and filling in the cells with plus or minus signs, as appropriate, one by one—ending dramatically with that large minus sign in the last cell (see Figure 1.1). PowerPoint presentations can help people understand by making both memory and processing easier for them.

Presentations that Are Clear and to the Point

Using the eight principles to accomplish the three essential goals— connecting with the audience, directing and holding attention, and promoting understanding and memory—is the foundation for a clear and compelling presentation. Each of these eight principles draws on facts about our mental processes. And each of these principles comes into play, singly or in combination, as we create different aspects of presentations in the following chapters.

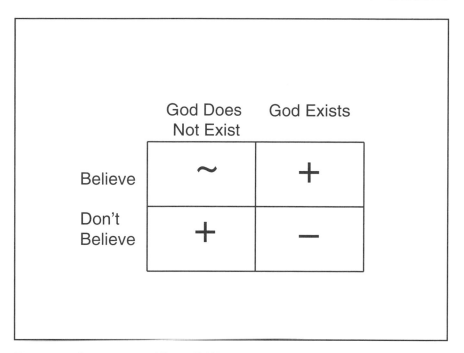

Figure 1.1. A summary of Pascal's Wager, which allows the audience easily to understand and retain the structure of the argument for believing in God.

In the remainder of the book, I will offer many specific recommendations based on these eight principles, some sweeping and some that may seem nit-picking—but all will help you to design and deliver compelling presentations. The principles apply at every level of scale, from the presentation as a whole all the way down to individual illustrations on a single slide and the design of a single bullet point.

Making Points in a PowerPoint Presentation: An Example

The hazards of not respecting the limitations of human mental processes are nicely illustrated—ironically—by one of Tufte's favorite graphics (Figure 1.2). This inventive graphic, created in 1861 by the French engineer Charles Joseph Minard, illustrates Napoleon's bold march to Moscow in 1812 and his dispirited retreat.

This display has never captivated me for the simple reason that— given human processing limitations—I needed several minutes to figure it out. I didn't realize initially that five different variables are being shown simultaneously (which violates the Principle of Capacity Limitations). For one, the width of the line represents the number of soldiers. And I didn't realize that time flows in both directions, left-to-right for the march to Moscow and vice versa for the march back (the lower line). (In our

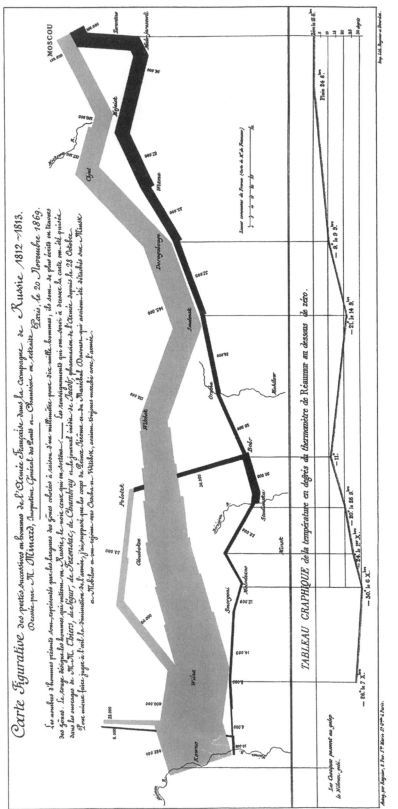

Figure 1.2. Minard's depiction of Napoleon's 1812 Russian campaign (from Tufte, 1983). See also color version, in insert.

culture, time is usually illustrated left to right, and thus the reverse violates the Principle of Compatibility.) Moreover, it took me a while to realize that the line indicating the retreat is indexed by a temperature scale, and I had trouble reading the small numbers that are at odd angles (which presumably indicate the numbers of surviving soldiers; both problems reflect violations of the Principle of Capacity Limitations).

I agree that M. Minard was amazingly clever and managed to cram a huge amount of information into a single display, but I can't agree that this is an effective way to communicate; the display doesn't present the facts so that they're clear or easily absorbed. If you are in the mood, you may enjoy taking the time to study the display for the fun of solving a puzzle, pondering intricate details, or appreciating the graphic devices employed. But if you want the facts and want them in a clear, easily understood way, this display is not the solution.

If you use the eight principles to take advantage of the features of the PowerPoint program, you could create a graphic that would save the viewer a lot of time and trouble: For example, first you could show just the line that represents the march to Moscow (and thereby exploit the Principles of Relevance and Salience). To make obvious the idea of movement over time, you could use animation to extend the line (relying on the Principle of Compatibility). Instead of a solid line, you could use dots—perhaps one for each 1,000 men, arranged into rows (making use of the Principles of Perceptual Organization), marching onward. On the next slide, you could gray out this material, so that it becomes the background for another line, fewer dots wide, moving back to France (thereby exploiting both the Principles of Salience and Discriminability). Indeed, this line could move more slowly (using a sequence of slides to produce variations in the speed of the animation, perhaps using the "custom animation" feature of the PowerPoint program for each horizontal segment), if the return march took more time—which would provide more information than the original, static display. In short, the PowerPoint program would let you direct the viewers' attention to one aspect of the display at a time, emphasize what's important by making the line more distinct than the background, use motion to capture the viewers' attention, and add information—and thus this presentation would be far more effective than the original.

How to Use This Book

Read the chapters in order to open your eyes to a whole new way of making and delivering PowerPoint presentations. Then read the appendix for enough information about the principles to apply them to your every situation.

What's in this Book

The following overview will help you organize what you read in the following chapters.

Chapter 2: Presentations that Work

The next chapter presents a sample PowerPoint presentation (that happens to show how the eight psychological principles can be used to make good graphs). You'll see how to apply the principles to the presentation as a whole: how to organize a presentation to connect with the audience, direct and hold attention, and promote understanding and memory.

Chapter 3: Legible Text

We next turn to the nitty-gritty of how to prepare individual slides. Here, you'll get guidelines for the appropriate sizes and fonts of text, and the use of bulleted lists. You'll also find out when to use tables and how to construct them so that they convey information effectively.

Chapter 4: Color, Texture, Animation, and Sound

Color, texture, animation (i.e., movement on the screen), and sound can bring a presentation to life and emphasize or enhance specific aspects of your message. Used incorrectly, however, they can distract and can bury specific aspects of your message. You'll see here how to use color to highlight material, convey information, and organize the display effectively. You'll also learn which colors tend to work well together and which don't, and what emotional associations specific colors convey. Then you'll learn how to use texture variations (in figure and background) and animation. And you'll learn the pro's and con's of adding specific types of soundtracks to your presentations.

Chapter 5: Communicating Quantitative Information: Graphs

Graphs are pictures that convey information about quantities. Because well-constructed graphs can communicate a lot of information quickly and effectively (perhaps even being worth the proverbial 1,000 words), they often are used in presentations. You'll see when to use graphs and which sort to use to illustrate a given type of data, to make a specific point, and to connect with a specific audience. You'll also get guidelines for how to make different sorts of graphs.

Chapter 6: Communicating Qualitative Information: Charts, Diagrams, Maps, Photographs, and Clipart

Some types of graphics—such as organizational charts and process diagrams—do not convey quantitative information. But the same principles that apply to quantitative graphs will also help you create effective qualitative graphics. You'll also see how to choose an appropriate icon or illustration, and when such visual aids will drive a point home or just drive the viewer to distraction.

Chapter 7: The Good, the Bad, and the Incomprehensible

In this final chapter, I begin by taking a single display that was once a candidate to be on every food item in the United States and analyze it using the eight principles. This analysis illustrates the power of the recommendations reviewed in the previous pages. Then we'll look at problems with certain features of the PowerPoint program, including cases when defaults either aren't helpful or are downright destructive. We'll finish by coming back to Tufte's attack on the PowerPoint program. I defend the potential of the medium and urge the reader not to blame the messenger medium for bad messages.

Appendix: Psychological Principles and Their Specific Aspects

Here you'll get a more detailed treatment of the principles, which provides you with enough information to apply them to all aspects of presentations.

From the Principles to the Point

At the end of each chapter I summarize the major points by bringing them back to the principles. This allows me to avoid citing the individual principles repeatedly in the body of the text and also reinforces the crucial role the principles play in these recommendations.

In this chapter, you saw that an effective presentation accomplishes three goals: It connects with the audience, directs and holds attention, and promotes understanding and memory. You also learned that this book presents a set of specific recommendations for achieving these goals; these recommendations are grounded in principles about the operation of the mental processes that underlie perception, memory, comprehension, cognition, emotion, and motivation. Each subsequent goal draws on the previous principles as well as any additional ones.

My advice focuses on how to structure your presentation so that your audience will receive and retain your message. Although there are no formulae that guarantee that you will convince your audience,

I can tell you this: If you ignore the three goals and the eight principles, you may as well be getting ready to run a foot race with one leg tied behind your back.

The three goals and principles that address them are as follows; each goal draws on the previously mentioned principles as well as the ones added specifically to address that goal.

Goal 1: Connect with your audience

Principle 1: The Principle of Relevance
Communication is most effective when neither too much nor too little information is presented.

Principle 2: The Principle of Appropriate Knowledge
Communication requires prior knowledge of relevant concepts, jargon, and symbols.

Goal 2: Direct and hold attention

Principle 3: The Principle of Salience
Attention is drawn to large perceptible differences.

Principle 4: The Principle of Discriminability
Two properties must differ by a large enough proportion or they will not be distinguished.

Principle 5: The Principle of Perceptual Organization
People automatically group elements into units, which they then attend to and remember.

Goal 3: Promote understanding and memory

Principle 6: The Principle of Compatibility
A message is easiest to understand if its form is compatible with its meaning.

Principle 7: The Principle of Informative Changes
People expect changes in properties to carry information.

Principle 8: The Principle of Capacity Limitations
People have a limited capacity to retain and to process information, and so will not understand a message if too much information must be retained or processed.

The Big Picture

Part of becoming senior in an organization is the privilege of running meetings. When I reached this developmental milestone, I soon learned always to prepare a detailed written agenda before each meeting. That preparation forced me think about both the process and possible outcomes of the meeting. For example, I discovered that the order of the agenda items was crucial: The discussion went much more smoothly if I put the easy items first so we had clearly accomplished at least something by the time the meeting ended.

The more difficult items often could be discussed indefinitely, as everyone realized, and by putting them at the end I could impose a deadline, which helped to focus the discussion. Designing the agendas properly usually allowed me to respect a one-hour rule: Sixty-one minutes spent in a meeting was often one minute too many. (Although even here, the Abraham Lincoln length-of-legs rule applied: If a meeting really required more time, more time it got.)

Designing a visual presentation is in some ways like designing the agenda for a meeting. You need to organize it so that you can ease the audience into the flow, and you need to know how to end it crisply. However, unlike many meetings, a presentation should have a single overarching theme and grand mission, supported by all its parts. The theme—the "Big Picture"—should be explicit from the outset, and you should use it to organize all that follows.

In this chapter we consider how to prepare a presentation. From the outset, you need to keep in mind that you are preparing a *presentation*—not an article, not a written report. Apparently, the United States military recently has not always made this distinction and actually used PowerPoint presentations in lieu of formal battle plans! This is an error. A presentation lacks the detail and precision of a written report, which makes it inappropriate for this role. But if you want to engage the audience and clearly convey key ideas and a handful of specific points, then a multimedia PowerPoint presentation can be just what you need.

8 Guidelines for the Overall Structure of Your Presentation

Eight is an important number, and not just because of the eight psychological principles I've summarized. The Buddhists speak of the "eight-fold path to enlightenment," there are eight cardinal directions on the compass, icons on a computer screen traditionally are multiples of eight pixels wide, and so on. In the following section I'm going to suggest another reason why eight is an important number. I'll offer eight guidelines for building presentations that communicate your message effectively.

1. Prepare to speak to a particular audience.

To make your message relevant to your audience, tailor your presentation to their knowledge, beliefs, and goals. To do so, you must find out what information is important to them and which level of presentation is appropriate for them. I was at a wedding reception recently, and while we were anxiously waiting to attack the huge and sumptuous cake, one of the guests gave a 15-minute toast, detailing how the happy couple met and what each of them said during their first date, and even a few embarrassing details of what they thought *after* the first date. For most of the other guests, this was TMI (Too Much Information).

How can you get to know your audience before you prepare your presentation?

- In many cases, this is easy: The audience members belong to a specific group, which almost by definition has specific knowledge and interests.
- If you can't fathom their interests from knowing the nature of their group, the first thing to do is simply to ask the events' organizer about the expected attendees. Find out what they do for a living, what sort of background they have, and what they are likely to want to know.
- What do you do if your audience includes people who have a range of backgrounds and interests? My advice is to aim for the middle range, but add some information (on a slide, or in a paraphrase) specifically aimed at the lower and higher ends. Avoid going for the lowest common denominator, which will only bore most of the audience.

2. Show and tell.

There's a reason that your elementary school teachers had you "show and tell." Different parts of the brain deal with language and with vision, and we humans store the two sorts of memories separately. When you present information both visually and verbally, you have two chances to get that material into the memory banks of your audience's minds.

So, combine graphics and text whenever possible to

- help the audience remember what you are saying.
- engage the audience's attention by providing visual variety. We notice what's different—and don't notice what's the same. So seeing a variety of visuals will keep your audience's interest and attention. Video clips can be even more effective, because of the added dimensions of movement and sound (see Chapter 3).

3. Plan in advance how you will direct the audience's attention.

Controlling what the audience looks at and listens to will maximize the chances that they will follow you. To do so:

- Each slide should contain only as much as you can read aloud or describe in about one minute. If you present too much text or too many graphics, the audience will be looking at one thing while you are saying another.
- Vary the salience of what you show by making what's important perceptually distinct. Capture the audience's attention by making important elements larger, brighter, or louder, so that you control what the audience members pay attention to.
- How you highlight your material should depend on the type of material you are highlighting: If you want the viewers to understand a complex structure (e.g., an organizational chart), it makes sense to build up a slide one part at a time, only showing the part you want to talk about at that moment. If you simply want them to focus on a specific part, it makes sense to "build a pointer" into your slide by including a red arrow that points to the subject of interest, or put a circle around a portion of a graphic or text that is your focus.

4. Don't lose your basic message by providing either too much or too little information.

Keep your eye on the ball: Remember what message you want to communicate, and what the audience members should take away with them when they leave the room. Provide no more and no less information than is needed to accomplish this goal. The usual temptation is to provide more information than is necessary to make your point, which is not a good idea for at least two reasons:

- By forcing the audience to *search for* what is important, you prevent them from devoting their full resources to *processing* it.
- You may tax the audience to the point that they simply tune you out.

In cutting out irrelevant detail, be careful not to discard crucial aspects of your material. Cut to the bone, but not into it.

5. Prepare your slides to function as your notes; don't rely on your memory.

Giving a presentation is anxiety provoking—I speak from experience, having given many hundreds of presentations and still feeling a bit anxious before giving one. Being in this anxious state makes it hard to keep in mind the points you need to make. So:

- Prepare the presentation so that you can use it as a memory aid. Include a slide that states every point you want to make. Use titles and graphics to prompt you to discuss specific ideas.
- The more familiar you are with the material, the more abbreviated these prompts can be. But don't abbreviate the material on the slides to the point that it won't make sense to the audience. The slides that prompt you should also underline key points for the audience to help them easily comprehend and remember.
- Yes, the PowerPoint program does provide tools that allow you to see notes that are not projected to the audience, but I advise that you avoid using them, for two reasons:

    1. You need to be relatively near your computer's screen to read them. And because we humans are incredibly good at spotting the target of another person's gaze, the audience will see you looking down at your computer, not at them or at the image projected on the screen that they see. The audience will tend to look where you look, so they will be looking at the back of your computer, rather than at the screen. The audience might also feel that you are ignoring them.
    2. By not sharing the information you are using to give the presentation, you may be saving the best stuff for yourself. Let the audience use your prompts to help them organize and remember what you show and tell.

6. Use the full range of communication options.

Some types of material or topics do not lend themselves well to bulleted lists or even graphics and videoclips. For example, there is a famous parody of a PowerPoint presentation in which the Gettysburg Address is reduced to six slides (see www.norvig.com/Gettysburg/sld001.htm). This medium is not meant to replace other forms of communication but rather to add to them. Telling a personal anecdote that has a crisp bottom line may be far more effective in some cases than listing the key points—or even presenting an illustrated version. In these cases, use the PowerPoint tools to

- structure your presentation.
- allow the audience to see how what you present fits into the structure.
- prompt you to present the anecdote by providing a title, such as "An Unlikely Story and a Moral," perhaps with an appropriate graphic, to cue you to tell your tale.

7.   Build in breaks that allow the audience to "come up for air".

In the South of France, home of foie gras, the farmers put funnels down the throats of ducks and force-feed them until their livers grow large and fatty. The ducks probably don't like this treatment, and audiences definitely don't like being given the equivalent in a presentation. So, give the audience time to digest what you've said. You can do this in two ways:

- Break up the information with a cartoon, joke, or demonstration. But if you use a joke, be careful: First, as the vampire bats showed you in Chapter 1, the joke must relate to the topic of your presentation. Second, avoid jokes about politics, race, or religion (your mother probably told you this, and she was right). Avoid making fun of your audience. Lawyer jokes are almost always safe— unless, of course, you are speaking to lawyers.
- Show an entertaining video clip that illustrates your point by reinforcing information you've already provided.

8.   Prepare for questions.

One of the worst fates a speaker can suffer is when the question period at the end is met with dead silence; we all know that this does not show that the audience was bowled over and is now utterly convinced. I gave a presentation this year that was followed by an open-ended question period; after an hour and 10 minutes, the moderator cut it off. I considered this vigorous discussion a sign that the presentation was a resounding success: Questions mean that you engaged the audience enough that they thought about the material and want feedback regarding connections they've made or want more information. If you've given your presentation well, you should expect questions.

- Master the material. Be able to explain exactly what is on every slide.
- Anticipate questions that might come up in the question period and reserve some slides to help answer them. (You no doubt will have more to say than you can fit into your presentation and thus can use the question period to slip in additional points.) The hyperlink feature of the PowerPoint program lets you turn any object on a slide into a button link to any other slide. So, you can define a button on the final slide in advance, to take you to your reserved slides whenever the audience is ready for them.

- If nobody immediately steps up to the plate with the first question, be patient. If you are still standing expectantly with a pleasant expression on your face after 20 or 30 seconds and there still are no takers, you might make a little joke such as "I hope I wasn't skating fast on thin ice" or "Should I be taking this as a testament to my powers of persuasion?" But don't fear: Social pressure alone will produce the first question, and more will follow.

The previous eight recommendations apply to the presentation as a whole as well as to each of its sections—the introduction, body, and wrap-up. Now, we'll turn to guidelines that apply to the individual sections themselves.

Building the Introduction

An effective presentation has a clear structure, with each part's having a distinct focus that clearly relates to the other parts. Think of the overall structure of your presentation as a pair of bookends flanking a set of books: The first bookend is the introduction; the books themselves are the body of the presentation; and the final bookend is the wrap-up. We begin at the beginning, with the introduction. An important fact about human memory is that we remember best the beginning and end of a sequence, so the beginning and end of your presentation are particularly important.

To illustrate the power of the principles, I'll give examples of key parts of a presentation I've prepared on how to construct effective graphs.

1.   Start with a bang.

A president of the United States may have a 100-day honeymoon period after taking office, but as a speaker you'll be lucky if you have even a five-minute grace period after taking the podium, during which the audience is willing to give you the benefit of the doubt and listen. If during this period you don't convince the audience that you have something of value to say, you will be likely to lose them.

- Your very first slide should define the topic and set the stage for your presentation. To do so, it can simply provide a title, your name, your affiliation, and any other vital information. (For details about titles, see Chapter 3.)
- One way to construct an effective opening has two distinct phases:

1. Prepare a graphic slide that not only defines the topic, but also sets the emotional stage; this slide can be visible before you take the podium, greeting attendees when they walk into the room. For example, if you are talking about dwindling oil reserves, you could use a picture of oil fields burning in Iraq.

2. Prepare a second slide that is identical to the first, except that the background is very low contrast and the title of your presentation, your name, and your affiliation are superimposed in clearly discriminable type. To begin your presentation, you can fade the first slide into the second (using the fade transition that is available in the PowerPoint program), which is an effective way to grab the attention of the audience so that they notice the additional information. Be sure the background of the second slide is very low contrast, to make the text stand out.

Example: Figures 2.1 and 2.2 are adapted from a presentation I've given on the principles summarized in Chapter 1, as applied to designing graphs per se. In the first slide, I provided the title of the presentation and my affiliation; given the topic, I opted not to begin with a fancy graphic—a clean and simple look is most compatible with the subject matter. In the second slide, I presented an example that both grabs the attention of the audience and provides a very general orientation to the topic ("Les Papillion D'Anna," http://kss.free.fr/0kssgallery.htm, email: kss@free.fr). I point out that computers now allow people to make displays very easily, for better or worse. I also point out that what I'll be talking about are all psychological issues—many of which have to do with how we perceive and understand what we see. I note that if the point were to communicate, there would be three problems with the slide I present: (1) It is difficult to tell what is being shown because the contrast is poor; (2) it is hard to organize the image into coherent shapes because the colors are not sharply defined; and (3) moreover, without knowing the context, it is difficult to know why certain features are included while others are not. What do those birds mean, anyway? And is that really a giant squid in the background? If nothing else, this initial exercise intrigues and draws in the audience.

2.   Build on the audience's knowledge and concerns when you explain why your topic is important.

The next slide or slides should tell the audience why they should pay attention to what you have to say. These slides should define the topic of your presentation, and then set you up to explain why your

Graph Design for the Eye and Mind

Stephen M. Kosslyn

Harvard University

Figure 2.1. A title slide, which conveys the key information about the topic and presenter. Please note that the illustrations in this book can only approximate how slides will look when projected by a particular projector. So there is no substitute for actually viewing a presentation as it will appear to the audience before delivering it, and adjusting contrast and color as necessary.

Figure 2.2. An opening slide that engages the audience. Although this is a work of art, one can ask how it would function to communicate a specific message and point out some of the problems with using it in this way. ("Les Papillons d'Anna," reprinted with permission from Kss. See color version in insert.)

topic is important to your audience. Tap into what your audience already knows and believes.

> **Example:** In my presentation, I needed to tell my audience the point (Figure 2.3), and then immediately acknowledge that people sometimes have the *wrong idea* of what a psychological principle is; they think it has something to do with psychotherapy or Freud. To disabuse them of this idea, I prepared a slide with a cartoon of a person on a couch during psychoanalysis, with a large red circle that has a slash through it (Figure 2.4). The slide following the cartoon prompts me to explain what I mean by the term "psychological principle" (Figure 2.5).

3. Define the topic by providing a concrete example.

Following the initial slides, present graphics or anecdotes that illustrate your topic. If need be, use two or three slides, which can contain any type of graphics (including cartoons), and you can also use sound as appropriate (for more detail, see Chapter 4).

> **Example:** In my presentation, I begin by showing the table in Figure 2.6 and ask whether any gender or income-level group

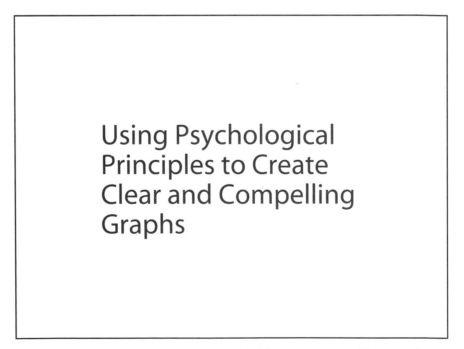

Figure 2.3. This slide introduces the topic of the presentation. The black frame helps to draw the viewers' attention to the text.

Figure 2.4. This slide acknowledges that many people have an overly narrow view of what psychology is and believe that it pertains only to psychotherapy. The audience needs to be disabused of this idea early in the presentation. (See also color version, in insert.)

Psychological Principles:
The nature of mental processes, such as those used in :

Perception
Memory
Cognition

Figure 2.5. After saying what psychology is not (i.e., entirely focused on psychotherapy), I need to add some of the things that it is; this slide prompts me to explain what I mean by the term "psychological principle."

Triglyceride Level by Income Group, Sex, and Age Group

INCOME GROUP	MALES		FEMALES	
	Under 65	65 or Over	Under 65	65 or Over
$0–24,999	250	200	375	550
$25,000+	430	300	700	500

Figure 2.6. To begin to illustrate the power of graphics, I present data in a table and ask whether any group (with group defined by the different combinations of gender and income level) shows different effects of age on triglyceride levels (these are fictional data).

shows different effects of age on triglyceride levels from the other groups. I let the audience ponder the table for four or five seconds (and it's clear from the looks on their faces that they can't tell), and then I present the graph in Figure 2.7. It is immediately evident from this graph that age affects females in the lowest income group in the opposite way from how it affects those in the other groups.

Question: Why is this conclusion so clear in the graph?

Answer: Because our visual systems are very good at detecting differences in the orientations of lines (especially when these differences are greater than 30 degrees of tilt—the difference between a clock's little hand pointing at 12 and big hand pointing at 1), and such differences convey the appropriate information here (which plays to the Principle of Perceptual Organization—specifically, the aspect of Input Channels, as summarized in the appendix).

4.   Tell the audience what you want them to conclude.

As part of the introduction, include material that explains what conclusions you are going to support. Prepare slides, video, sound—or

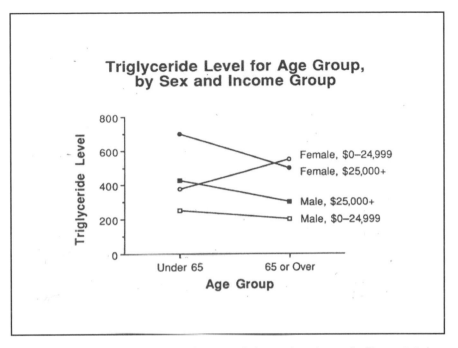

Figure 2.7. This graph presents the same information shown in Figure 2.6, but the atypical group now is obvious at first glance.

just a script for what you will say aloud. That will pique the audience's interest, that will make them wonder how you will get from here to there.

Example: In my presentation, I prepared Figure 2.8 to demonstrate that graphs aren't better than tables in general. I point out that Figure 2.8 displays the identical data as Figure 2.7 but plotted differently; now it's not immediately clear which group deviates from the others. Then—as planned in advance—I ask, "Why not?"

This rhetorical question lets me tell the audience where I am going in the presentation. (The answer, by the way, is that our visual systems are not good at detecting *differences in differences* of height—and that's how the relevant information is conveyed in this particular graph. We humans are terrific at comparing differences in tilt, but not differences in differences of heights. But for all we know a Martian, with a different brain, might have the opposite strength and weakness.)

In setting up this sequence of slides, I've looked ahead to a key part of what I want the audience to conclude: Namely, that our ease in understanding the message in Figure 2.7 versus our difficulty with exactly the same information in Figure 2.8 reflects fundamental facts about how our perceptual systems work, not attributes of the figures or the data themselves.

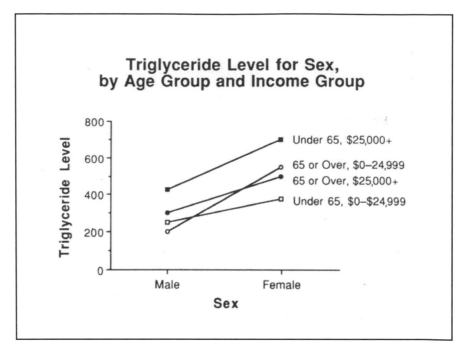

Figure 2.8. This graph presents the same information provided in Figures 2.6 and 2.7, but the atypical group is no longer obvious at first glance. The point: It's not that graphs are always better than tables; graphs are superior only when they play to our perceptual strengths—and avoid relying on our weaknesses. We are good at noticing differences in tilt (Figure 2.7), but not differences among differences in height (this graph).

5. Provide a road map.

If the structure of your argument involves making distinct points or addressing a set of related topics, avoid making your presentation one long string; organize it into digestible modules. And give the audience the conceptual structure of the major parts of your presentation so they can organize what you are going to say. Let them see the agenda. A *brief* outline is a good way to provide a conceptual structure. Organize your outline to reduce the load on your audience members' mental processes as much as possible. As I noted in Chapter 1, a presentation marches on over time; it is not like a written article or report that allows the reader to set his or her own pace and go back when desired. Thus, you need to help your audience follow along so they do not get lost, confused, or overwhelmed.

• The outline should make the structure of your presentation clear.

- Respect the *Rule of Four*. Organize your outline hierarchically into groups of no more than four pieces of information because that's about all we humans can hold in mind at the same time. Each of these groups, however, can in turn include up to four groups (but I don't recommend pushing to the limit—if possible, each group should contain no more than three pieces of information).
- After you present the outline of the major parts of your presentation, briefly explain what is in each part.

Example: In Figure 2.9, I made an outline of the major parts of my presentation on graphs, which focuses on the three goals that should be attained by an effective communication. (These are the same three goals I discussed in Chapter 1, applied to all aspects of presentations.) I explain that these three goals can be achieved by using eight major psychological principles.

Preparing the Body of the Presentation

The following 10 recommendations will help you prepare the body of your presentation.

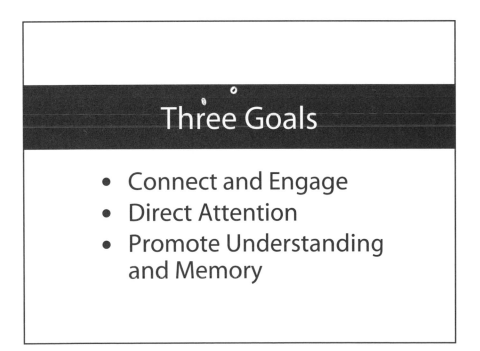

Figure 2.9. An outline of the three goals that will be addressed in the presentation; I briefly explain each one.

1.   Tell a story.

The human brain automatically tries to organize and make sense out of experience. One happy consequence of this tendency may be that humans like to tell and understand stories. Take advantage of this proclivity by telling a story in the body of your presentation. In order to do so:

- Create a clear line of argument from the beginning to the end of the body, along which you build a case for the conclusion or conclusions you want to draw.
- Ensure that the transitions between parts are clear.
- Organize the parts so that each provides the foundation for the next.

2.   Make a slide that draws attention to the first entry in your outline.

Because you have a story structure, it's important to have the audience members start at the beginning and then work their way through your points, seeing how each one follows from the previous points. Set up your initial slide in the body of the presentation to draw the audience's attention to the first item in your outline. One way to do this is to show the outline with all but the top entry grayed out. Graying out everything but one topic will lead your audience to focus on just the part that is relevant at the moment. Including the grayed out headings will let your audience gauge where you are in the presentation. You can also draw the audience's attention to the relevant part by making this material a different color or a bigger or italic font, have an arrowhead point to it, or make the relevant material slide in from the left.

Example: In Figure 2.10 of my presentation, I have grayed out everything but the topic I want to address in the following portion of the presentation.

3.   Prepare an outline for each part that has two or more subparts.

If each of your points needs to be unpacked, then divide each part of your presentation into subparts and introduce them in a mini-outline. Give the audience an organizational structure that will help

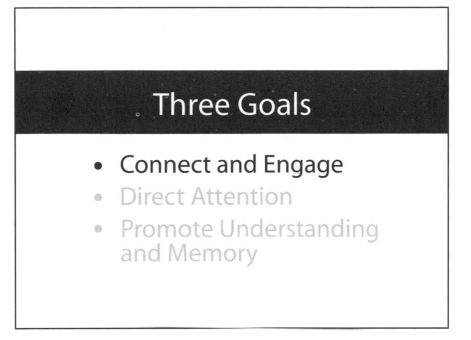

Figure 2.10. The same outline as in Figure 2.9, but with only the top entry salient. By graying out the other entries, I direct the audience members' attention to the relevant heading, which introduces the following section of the presentation.

them understand and remember both your entire presentation and the material you present in each part.

• As indicated in Figure 2.11, show that you're diving more deeply into the outline by reducing the salience of the heading, and by changing the color and the size of the text in the outline or by using different bullets, such as "●" for the first level and ">" for the second level.

Example: For the main outline, I've used 44-point white type in a black-filled text box for the top-level heading (Figure 2.9), and 36-point black type for the entries. The heading is thus clearly more salient than the entries. For the secondary (subpart) outline (Figure 2.11), I used the 36-point type for the heading, now white in a smaller (and hence less salient) black text box. In general, overall titles should be more salient than entries or titles for subparts. You can also vary salience by varying color. For example, in my presentations, I sometimes use a gray background with a very salient gold for the first-level headings, less-salient white for the next level down, and washed-out yellow for the third level. In all cases, however, the words are clearly discernable from the background.

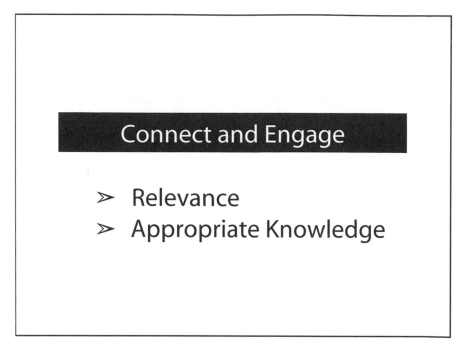

Figure 2.11. Because the following part is composed of two or more subparts, I present an outline of the subparts. As shown here, the names of the subparts should look distinctive and less salient than the name of the part itself.

4.   Prepare a slide to draw attention to the first subpart.

After presenting the outline that shows each subpart, ensure that your next slide will draw your audience's attention to the first subpart in the outline.

Example: In my presentation, I used the same technique to draw attention to parts of the presentation as a whole (as illustrated in Figure 2.10) as to its subparts, as shown in Figure 2.12.

5.   Define key terms.

I know it sounds trite and obvious, but you should "define your terms." (Do you remember President Clinton's reflections on the word "is," in connection with his unfortunate interactions with Ms. Lewinsky?) Sometimes a lot hinges on exactly what you mean.

- Especially be sure to define technical terms. (If you aren't likely to find it in the front section of *The New York Times*, it's a good candidate for being a "technical term".)

Figure 2.12. I introduce each subpart by graying out the others, leaving salient only the name of the subpart about to be discussed.

- Put the definitions in writing, to let viewers read them as well as hear you say them aloud, which gives the viewers two chances to understand and remember them.

  Example: In Figure 2.13 of my presentation, I provide in writing a definition for the first principle I discuss, the Principle of Relevance.

6. Provide concrete, specific evidence to support your conclusions.

As I've stressed, you must decide what message you want the audience members to take away from the presentation as a whole—and you must do the same thing for each part. Think of the story and how it unfolds. Only then can you know how to present clear, specific evidence to back up your message.

Example: In my presentation, I first present an example of when relevance may be violated, in Figure 2.14 (found at www.plotit.com/PLOTIT/PICTURES/GRAPH.GIF), and ask the audience in what circumstances this overwhelming slide would be

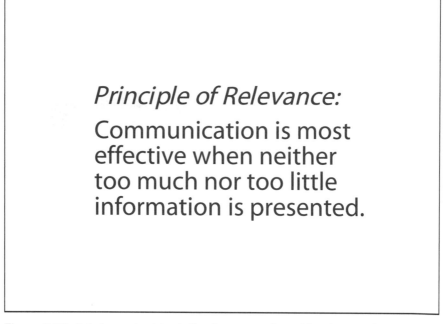

Figure 2.13. It is important to define key terms in writing (remember: use the slides as your notes), and read the definition aloud. This gives the audience two chances (visual and verbal) to absorb this crucial information.

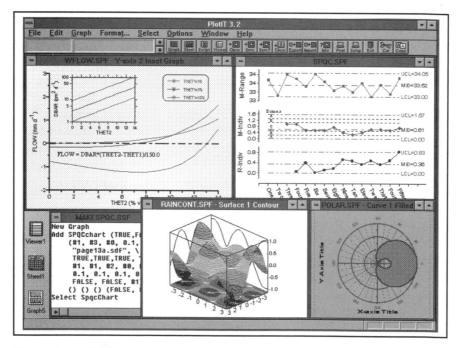

Figure 2.14. If this slide were used to convey specific data, it would provide too much information for the audience to absorb. To drive home this point, you could ask the audience to try to imagine in what situations so much information in such a complex display would be relevant. (Reprinted with permission by Scientific Programming Enterprises.)

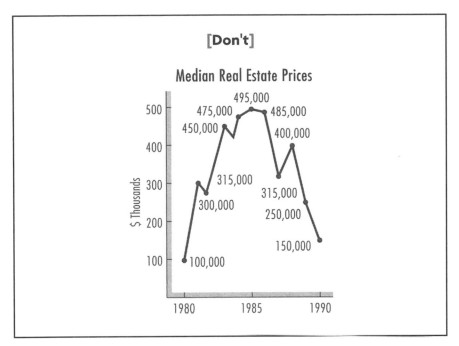

Figure 2.15. This graph illustrates a more common type of display that contains more information than can be absorbed easily. If it is intended to make a particular point, not all of this information is likely to be relevant.

appropriate (e.g., perhaps for marketing purposes, to illustrate what this software can do—we cannot dismiss even this display without knowing the context in which it is used). I then show them an example that presents too much information to illustrate peak and then-current real estate prices, Figure 2.15, and follow with an example that shows only the relevant material, Figure 2.16.

7. Conclude each part and subpart with a summary.

Even if the audience does not follow every word of every part and subpart of your presentation, a summary at the end of each part and subpart will give them the thrust of your presentation.

8. After each part or subpart, highlight the entry for the next part or subpart in the outline to signal its beginning.

Prepare a slide that will draw your audience's attention to the next topic on the outline.

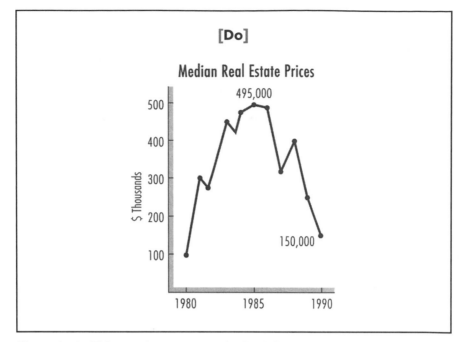

Figure 2.16. This graph presents only the information in Figure 2.15 that is relevant for the discussion, sparing the viewers from having to search for this information.

Example: In my presentation, I returned to the outline of the subparts, shown in Figure 2.11, and then I grayed out the top entry, leaving only the upcoming topic clearly shown. Similarly, after finishing that topic, I summarized it and then returned to the main outline, Figure 2.9. I then grayed out all but the heading for the following topic. Before continuing on to discuss this material, however, I inserted a transition slide, Figure 2.17, to remind my audience that the principles build on one another when they are used in the service of achieving certain goals.

In my actual presentation (not shown here), I then worked through the relevant subparts, which in turn explained and illustrated the Principles of Salience, Discriminability, and Perceptual Organization. Next, I returned to the main outline, and then grayed out all but the third goal. Following this, I presented an outline of the subparts, shown in Figure 2.18. This outline introduced the three relevant principles, the Principle of Compatibility, the Principle of Informative Changes, and the Principle of Capacity Limitations.

Let's pick this up at the end of the third subpart, where I turned to the Principle of Capacity Limitations, as shown in Figure 2.19.

Three Goals

Achieving additional goals is facilitated by additional principles, used in combination with the earlier ones.

Figure 2.17. Before moving to the material in the next major part, I present a transition slide to remind the audience that principles in the service of the first goal also help to accomplish the following goals.

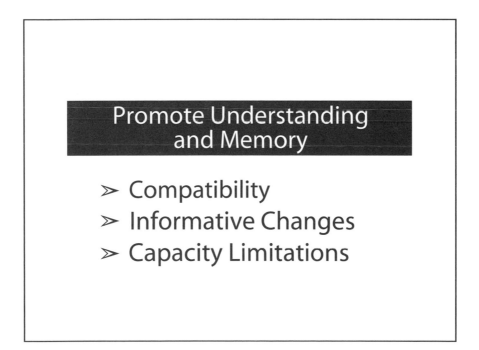

Figure 2.18. This slide shows the outline of the three subparts for the final major part of the presentation.

I defined the principle, Figure 2.20, and turned to one aspect of it, short-term memory limitations, in Figure 2.21.

9. Prepare demonstrations.

As you saw earlier, people automatically pay attention to things that are clearly different. And there is nothing more different than being asked suddenly to shift from being a passive listener to being an active participant. Plus, as you now know, actively processing information helps people understand and remember.

- To keep your audience alert and engaged, prepare a demonstration or even simply ask them to raise their hands if they agree (or disagree) with a specific point.

Example: In Figures 2.22 to 2.26 I have a demonstration of the Principle of Capacity Limitations, focusing on short-term memory limits. Here's how I set it up: When I present Figure 2.22, I read the slide aloud, telling the audience that I'll read a set of directions, such as the ones they are about to see. Then I show Figure 2.23,

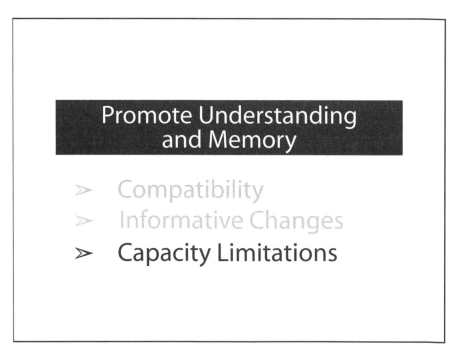

Figure 2.19. After presenting the material for each subpart, I revisited the outline of the subparts at its end, and then grayed out all but the heading that introduced the next subpart, working down the entries until the last one, shown here.

Principle of Capacity Limitations:

People have a limited capacity to retain and to process information, and will not understand a message if too much information must be retained or processed.

Figure 2.20. I again define the principle in writing and read this aloud.

One aspect of this principle:

Limited short-term memory capacity: We can hold in mind only about four units at the same time.

Figure 2.21. I now define a key aspect of the principle, and again read it aloud.

Capacity Limitations in Action :
A Demo!

You will soon hear a sequence of spatial directions (such as North, Northeast, Southeast), and should visualize a one-inch line segment for each one, oriented in the appropriate way, and connect each line to the previous one to form a pathway.

Figure 2.22. This slide summarizes the instructions for the demo, which I read aloud.

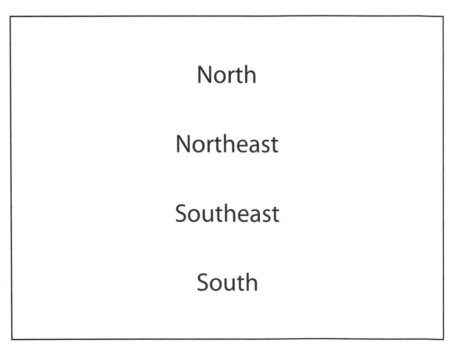

North

Northeast

Southeast

South

Figure 2.23. This slide illustrates the first step of a demonstration to illustrate key characteristics of our limited capacity short-term memories. I told the audience that I would read the directions one at a time, and they should visualize a one-inch line segment pointing in each direction, with each successive segment attached to the tail end of the previous one to form a pathway.

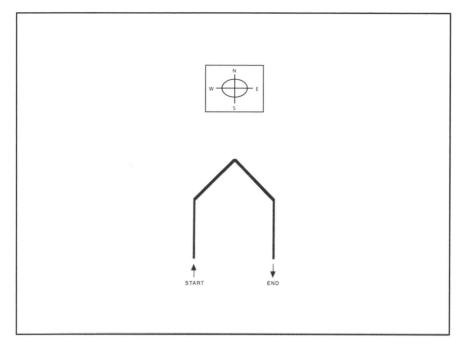

Figure 2.24. This slide illustrates the path that the audience should have visualized after receiving the directions in Figure 2.27. I used this and the previous slide to teach the audience the task and to give them a little practice before turning to the actual demonstration in the next two slides.

Northeast

Southeast

North

East

South

East

North

East

South

Northeast

Southeast

Figure 2.25. The actual test directions I used in this demonstration. The audience members were asked to close their eyes and visualize a line segment pointed in each direction, with each line in succession connected to the previous one to form a single pathway.

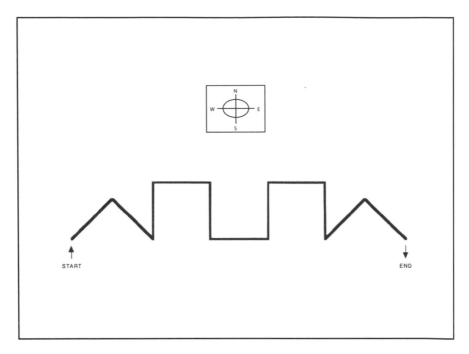

Figure 2.26. The pathway that the audience members should have visualized on hearing the directions in Figure 2.25. Only people who noticed the repeating patterns got this right, which illustrates that we can hold about four units in short-term memory, and that each of those units in turn can be composed of about four elements.

and tell them that I want them to visualize a one-inch line segment for each of these directions oriented in that direction, and to mentally connect each segment to the end of the previously specified one—creating a path of connected segments. Figure 2.24 illustrates the path that would have been formed by following the directions in Figure 2.23. I then ask whether there are any questions about what I'm asking them to do. When the task is clear, I ask them to close their eyes and visualize the pathway while I read aloud each direction in Figure 2.25. I use the PowerPoint program to show me the directions, one every 4 seconds, which is enough time for the audience to visualize the segment.

After reading the last direction, I ask the audience members to open their eyes and look at Figure 2.26 and to raise their hands if they were able to visualize it. Then—and this is the crucial part of the demonstration—I ask them to raise their hands if they noticed the repeating patterns, the peaked and square forms. Finally, I ask how many of those who "got it right" also noticed the patterns. Without fail, virtually all of the people who got it right also noticed the patterns. Why? Because the limit on short-term memory is not the number of *items* (the individual line segments, in this case)—it's the number of *units*. If audience members could figure out how to organize the segments into four or fewer units, they could store the entire set in short-term memory.

(In the presentation, I follow up this demonstration with a number of examples of graphs that exceed the limits of short-term memory, which I won't present here because I respect the Principle of Relevance—and the overview I've given is good enough for present purposes. In the actual presentation, I show multiple examples, and summarize by returning to the outline in Figure 2.27.)

10. Consider marking your progress with a banner or other signpost.

If your presentation must contain more than four parts or more than four subparts in a part (which, as noted earlier, I do not recommend—three is better still, posing no strain), let the audience know where you are. One way to do so is a banner across the top of each slide. This banner should give the names of the major part and subpart, using the same names as the outline, and make salient the name of

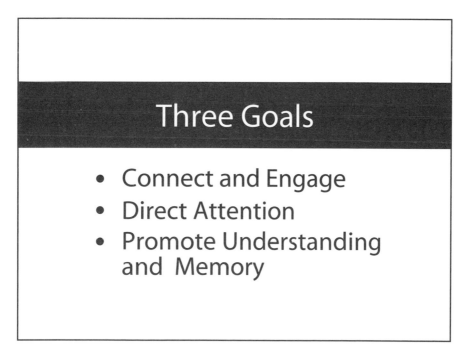

Figure 2.27. At the end of the presentation, I first return to the overall outline and briefly summarize the bottom line reached in each part.

the current topic. An alternative is to include a small box in the upper left or right that keeps track of your progress.

- Ensure that such a signpost is distinct from (i.e., is not grouped with) the other material on the slide by using a different font size or color; you also should make it less salient than the other material on the slide.

I do not include such a banner in my own presentation because many of my slides are so visually complex that they don't leave space (or processing capacity in the audience) for a banner.

Preparing the Wrap-up

My late colleague Roger Brown, whose book *Social Psychology* defined that field, once told me that a good presentation begins by explaining to the audience what you're going to tell them, then telling it to them, and then reminding them what you've just told them. Because people remember best the beginning and end of a sequence, the end of the presentation is very important. Here are three recommendations for the all-important wrap-up of your presentation.

1.   Repeat the opening outline.

Make a duplicate of the outline and use it to remind the audience what the presentation included.

Example: As shown in Figure 2.27, show the audience the outline of the major parts and briefly summarize verbally what you said and concluded in each part. In my presentation, I turned back to the eight principles, as shown in Figure 2.28.

2.   Prepare text and graphics to emphasize your conclusions.

Ask yourself: If your audience were to give a one- or two- sentence summary of your presentation to a friend, what would it be? Instead of trusting that summary to chance, give it directly. And instead of trusting to memory, prepare slides that make these crucial points.

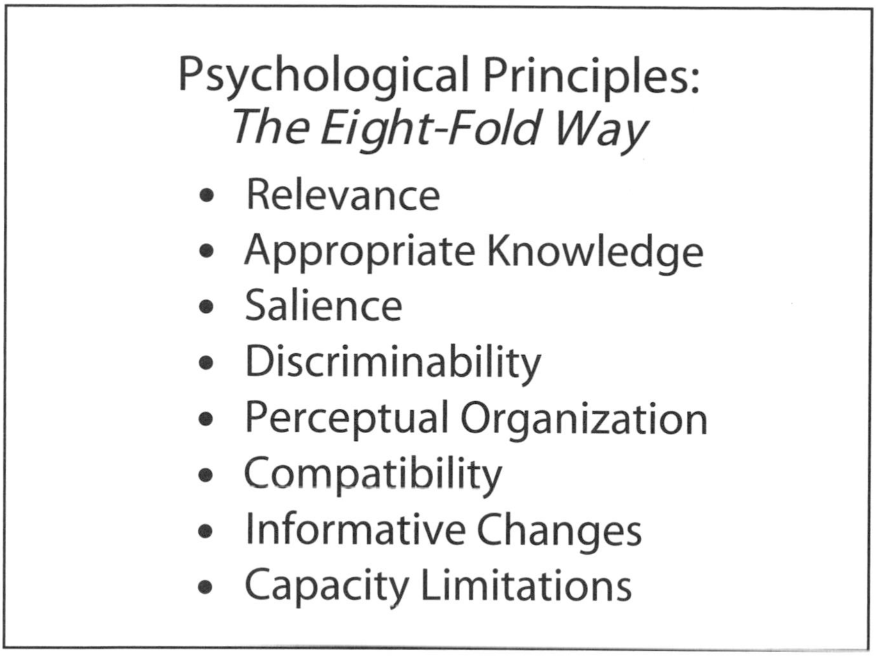

Psychological Principles:
The Eight-Fold Way

- Relevance
- Appropriate Knowledge
- Salience
- Discriminability
- Perceptual Organization
- Compatibility
- Informative Changes
- Capacity Limitations

Figure 2.28. In this presentation, I introduce the eight principles, and as part of the summary I briefly revisit each of them.

One way to give your audience the message directly is to return to the same graphics that you showed in the introduction, but now add some text or verbal explanation to help your audience see them "in a new light."

Example: In my presentation, I return to Figure 2.2 (repeated in Figure 2.29) and use the principles to explain why it is difficult (assuming that the designer intended it to communicate in the first place!). In an effort to turn a sow's ear into a silk purse, I use the fact that this is not a communication graphic, but rather a work of art, to my advantage—I point out the difference and underscore the importance of relevance.

3. **Set up a snappy ending.**

You should close crisply, to signal that you've put in place the final bookend. I can't count the number of times I've heard presentations that ended limply with a statement such as, "Well, that's it" or "OK, that's all I want to say," leaving the audience wondering whether more should have been said. An effective way to end with a snap is by using a graphic, or perhaps, even a well-chosen cartoon.

Figure 2.29. To help the audience "see in a new light," I return to the graphic that I used at the outset. I now explain *why* it would not serve to communicate well (assuming that it was ever intended to have that role, which is doubtful—in part because of the problems it would have if pressed into service in this way).

Example: The iconic pizza-pie graph in Figure 2.30 provided the snappy ending for my presentation when I explained it in terms of the principles. (I pointed out that removing one slice lets us distinguish the wedges because it disrupts the good continuation of the boundary, thereby creating another perceptual unit. Then I said, "I was surprised when I first learned that pizza provides a balanced, nutritious meal. I hope this presentation provided the balanced, essential ingredients for your presentations, and thank you for your time and attention."

Another, perhaps better, example: At the end of a presentation on the nature of mental imagery in which I stressed that we can have mental images from more than one of our senses ("seeing with the mind's eye," "hearing with the mind's ear," and so on), I showed a Dilbert cartoon. Dilbert was on a date. In the first panel, his date says, "I cannot begin to describe how I feel when I'm with you." ' Dilbert replies, "Try." In the next panel, she says, "Imagine a spring day, with bright flowers, birds singing and a gentle breeze." Dilbert is smiling. And then comes the last panel, in which she continues: "And now imagine a tractor on your

Figure 2.30. To end on a light note, and also to underscore the generality of the principles, I show this picture of a pizza pie, which serves to illustrate how some of the principles could turn this into a pie graph.

chest." After the audience laughed, I returned to the cartoon and noted the different modalities of mental imagery, the visual (flowers), auditory (birds), and tactile (breeze and tractor). I finished with a comment that the author of the cartoon was not only a keen observer of human relationships but also a perceptive observer of mental processing, having noticed these important aspects of mental imagery. I then thanked the audience for their attention.

Ending on a crisp note like that left a moment of silence, followed by a gratifying amount of applause (probably as much for my treatment of the cartoon as for the talk itself). (Note: If you have any doubt about whether it is appropriate to show or even describe a cartoon, give your lawyer a call—better safe than sued!)

At the very end, repeat your introductory slide (Figure 2.31, in my case), with the title of the presentation and your name—neatly putting in place the second bookend. If you leave this slide on the screen during the question period, it has the added benefit of helping the audience to stay on topic.

Figure 2.31. I end by returning to the opening slide, which not only reminds the audience of the topic and my identity, but also may help them stay on topic during the question session.

Getting the message across: Delivering the presentation

Because your presentations should be conceived and constructed from the outset to be delivered to an audience, this chapter would not be complete without a brief discussion of how to deliver presentations.

1.   Speak to—not at—your audience.

Keep in mind the three following recommendations.

1. Show only key words and phrases; don't show your audience every word you plan to say. I've seen presenters who did this, and they failed to control the attention of their audience— because the audience members were so busy reading that they didn't listen. And in order to fit every word on the screen, the presenter forced the audience to squint to see all that small print.

2. Speak conversationally; don't read your presentation word for word. Yes, what you have to say may require precise wording, and, yes, writing it out in advance and reading it is a security blanket. But these benefits are outweighed by this fact: Unless you've had acting lessons, you'll probably slip into reading in a droning monotone and may soon hear the gentle sounds of snoring. People expect perceptible differences when information is being conveyed; if the sounds stay the same (droning on), the audience members will have trouble staying attentive, let alone awake.

3. Monitor the audience; don't focus your attention solely on your notes and slides. Another problem with reading or focusing too closely on your notes is that you can't easily monitor the audience. You should look at the audience members so that you can vary the speed and level of your presentation based on feedback you pick up. If you catch puzzled looks, slow down and clarify your points; if the audience seems restless and bored, speed up. As Yogi Berra put it, "You can observe a lot by just watching."

2.   Face the audience.

Your mother probably told you never to turn your back on people. She was right again; this is good advice and not simply from the point of view of politeness. People can't hear you as well when you talk to the wall, and they can't read your expressions or your lips when they can't see you. And you can't read the audience. So:

- Stand to the side of the screen when you read from it, turning to look out at the audience after reading each point.
- Make sure that you aren't standing in the dark. Dim the lights to the point that your slides are easy to see, but leave enough light for the audience to see your face and gestures (which are another way we communicate, indicating what's most important and most relevant).
- If you expand verbally on material you have presented, move around the stage as you talk, which will keep the audience's attention on you. But stop moving as soon as you present a new slide, video, or audio file. Don't make the audience choose between paying attention to you versus your new material! And never pace, which is always distracting.

3.   Don't rush it.

Unless you are the leader of an authoritarian regime (in the Fidel Castro tradition), you probably have a limited amount of time in which to give your presentation. Thus, you might be tempted to try to cram in as much as possible by talking as quickly as possible. Clamp down on this impulse! Talking quickly and reviewing material quickly can convey the sense of "skating fast over thin ice." Your presentation will be compelling only if it's clear that you have mastery of the material, which is not obvious if you rush.

- Set a speaking pace that lets audience members understand one sentence before you begin to say the next. (Otherwise, you'll overload their limited processing capacity.)
- Give the audience enough time to take in each slide.
- Don't "talk over" the text you show, saying one thing while the audience tries to read another. As I mentioned in Chapter 1, a presentation is no place for a Stroop Effect.
- You don't need to read every slide title aloud if you leave enough time for the audience to read. But do read the most important material aloud to give the audience two ways—visual and verbal—to store it.

4.   Know what you can skip.

There's no point in being right on time if you pitched your presentation at too high a level or compressed it too much for the audience, so that much of what you had to say whizzed by them. To avoid either situation:

- Say at the outset that you'll be happy to take *questions of clarification* during the presentation, but would prefer that the audience hold other questions until the end. Such a statement can allow you to stay on time and avoid being derailed by contentious or complex questions. This invitation will also allow you to identify and clarify misconceptions at the outset (it is sometimes surprising how ideas that people bring to a particular topic can lead them to misunderstand what is being said, so it is useful for you to clear the air as early as possible). Moreover, asking the audience to defer general questions immediately after you've invited other sorts of questions softens any sense that you are trying to muzzle them.
- Alternatively, you may be comfortable interrupting the flow and answering all types of questions as they arise, which will make the audience feel that they are being listened to. However, this generous impulse must be managed or the structure of your carefully constructed presentation could be ripped to shreds, which is neither in your nor your audience's interest.
- Keep in mind that you can't always anticipate how long your presentation will take. For one thing, you'll be monitoring the faces and nonverbal signs of the audience and adjusting your pace appropriately. For another, being asked to clarify something will slow you

down. Decide ahead of time what material you can skip through quickly, in case you find that you're running out of time. If necessary, you can tell your audience that you'll go quickly over a section because you've determined that it's less relevant to their needs. Then present the slides in that part very briefly, dwelling only on the concluding slide while explaining what the previous slides led up to.

5.   Respond to questions.

As noted earlier, you should have prepared for questions. When you receive them:

- Don't feel that you must answer every question on the spot. Sometimes (rarely) a member of the audience hits on a point that you (the expert) might not have considered. In such cases, if you don't immediately know how to answer, simply say "That's an excellent question. Rather than throwing out my first take and giving you a glib response, let me have a few minutes to think about this." Everyone likes being acknowledged publicly as smart, and this response will come off much better than a rambling, nondefinitive response—which could undermine your credibility in general. In fact, you may even wish to speak to the individual after your presentation and say that you'll need to do some research and will send him or her an e-mail in a day or two to answer. There's no shame in not knowing everything there is to know.
- Always repeat each question as soon as it is asked, so that everyone in the entire room can hear it. Many members of the audience may not hear questions directed at the speaker, particularly if the questioner is near the front of the room. Repeating the questions not only ensures that everyone knows why you'll address a specific point, but it gives you a moment to gather your wits and think about what you should say!
- Close the question period by thanking the audience for their time and attention and for giving you the chance to talk to them. And then say "Thanks again" or make some other positive comment, with a smile and a nod—allowing you to leave the stage on a positive note.

From the Principles to the Point

The eight psychological principles give us plenty of guidance for organizing a presentation. In this chapter you saw guidelines for the overall structure of your presentation as well as guidelines for the introduction, body of the presentation, and the wrap-up. But in the face of all of these recommendations, I need to emphasize one thing, illustrated by this joke (www.nursinghumor.com/ humor/ lawyer.attorney.legal.a.lawyer.to.the.end.htm):

A lawyer was on his deathbed in his bedroom, and he called to his wife. She rushed in and said, "What is it, honey?" He asked her to run and get the Bible as soon as possible. Being a religious woman, she thought this was a good idea. She ran and got it, prepared to read him his favorite verse or something of the sort. He snatched it from her and began quickly scanning pages, his eyes darting right and left. The wife was curious, so she asked, "What are you doing, honey?" "I'm looking for loopholes!" he shouted.

I remind you that these recommendations are guidelines, not hard-and-fast rules. As long as you respect the eight psychological principles, you can look for loopholes. Here's a review of the recommendations I made in this chapter, in the context of the principles so that you can see where they came from. (I list each recommendation only under the principle that primarily motivated it, although in many cases more than one principle underlies the recommendation.)

Principle of Relevance: Communication is most effective when neither too much nor too little information is presented. (We understand and remember a message more easily when the right amount of detail is used to make the point.)

- Start with a bang; your very first slide should define the topic and set the stage for your presentation.
- Decide what message you want the viewers to take away from the presentation as a whole—and do the same thing for each part and subpart.
- Provide information only when it is needed.
- Don't lose your basic message by providing either too much or too little information; be sure not to swamp the audience with irrelevant detail.
- Include a slide that explicitly states every point you need to make.
- In general, the amount of text you present should just be enough to remind you to present the key points and give the audience a way to conceptualize what you're saying.
- Prepare for questions; hold some slides in reserve, in anticipation of specific questions.
- Don't ignore the audience; monitor them so that you can adjust your presentation.
- Know what you can skip.

- Respond to questions, but don't feel that you must answer every question on the spot.
- Wait 20 or 30 seconds after opening the question session, and if nobody has spoken up, make a self-deprecating comment or ask a rhetorical question (such as, "Was I skating too fast over thin ice?").

Principle of Appropriate Knowledge: Communication requires prior knowledge of pertinent concepts, jargon, and symbols. (We understand and remember a message more easily if it connects to what we already know.)

- Prepare to speak to a particular audience.
- Build on the audience's knowledge and concerns when you explain why your topic is important; find out what information is important to the audience, and which level of presentation is appropriate for them.
- Speak to—not at—your audience; for example, aim for the middle range, with occasional additional information (on a slide, or in a paraphrase) specifically aimed at the lower or higher end.
- Define the topic by providing a concrete example. Explain clearly and concisely why your topic is important to your audience.
- Define key terms, particularly if a term is being used in a technical sense.

Principle of Salience: Attention is drawn to large perceptible differences. (Big relative differences grab attention.)

- Plan in advance how you will direct the audience's attention.
- Capture the audience's attention by making different elements larger, brighter, or louder, so that you have absolute control over what the audience members pay attention to.
- Each slide should contain only what you can read aloud in about one minute.
- Make a slide that draws attention to the first entry in your outline.
- Prepare a slide to draw attention to the first subpart.
- After each part or subpart, highlight the entry for the next part or subpart in the outline.
- To direct attention to specific portions of a slide, build up a slide one part at a time or "build a pointer" into your slide.
- Prepare demonstrations; people automatically pay attention to things that are different, and they remember information best when they process it thoroughly.
- Don't print out your whole presentation and read it word for word (you will probably read in a monotone, which lulls attention).
- If you expand verbally on material you present, move around the stage to keep the audience's attention—but stop moving as soon as you present a new slide, video, or audio file. And never pace.

Principle of Discriminability: Two properties must differ by a large enough proportion or they will not be distinguished. (We need contrast to distinguish shapes, colors, or positions from each other and from the background.)

- Don't show your audience so much text that you will have to make the font very small.
- Face the audience.
- Stand to the side of the screen when you read from it, looking out at the audience after you read each point; they can see the screen better and hear you better.
- Make sure that you aren't standing in the dark.
- Always repeat each question as soon as it is asked so the entire room can hear it.

Principle of Perceptual Organization: People automatically group elements into units, which they then attend to and remember. (These groups are easier to see and remember than the isolated components would be.)

- Ensure that each signpost is clearly distinct from (i.e., is not grouped with) the other material.

Principle of Compatibility: A message is easiest to understand if its form is compatible with its meaning. (For better or worse, the mind tends to judge a book by its cover.)

- Use the full range of communication options.
- If you want the viewers to see how a portion is integrated into a whole, build it up in a series of slides.
- Don't "talk over" the text you show, saying one thing while the audience tries to read another.
- Don't talk quickly and review material quickly, which can convey the sense of "skating fast over thin ice."

Principle of Informative Changes: People expect changes in properties to carry information. (And we expect every necessary piece of information to be indicated by a change in a perceptible property.)

- Use a consistent and distinctively formatted slide to signal the beginning of each new part and subpart.
- Close with a crisp ending, which clearly signals that you've put in place the final bookend.

Principle of Capacity Limitations: People have a limited capacity to retain and to process information and so will not understand a message if too much information must be retained or processed. (From a communicative point of view, less can be more!)

- Prepare your slides to function as your notes; the slides that you use to jog your memory will also help the audience organize in their minds what you say, so that they can easily comprehend and remember.
- Show and tell: Use graphics in combination with text whenever possible.
- Tell the audience what you want them to conclude; as part of the introduction, explain where you are going in your presentation and what conclusions you are going to support.
- Provide a road map: Organize your outline to reduce the load on your audience members' attention, memory, and reasoning as much as possible.
- Your conceptual structure and outline should be organized hierarchically into groups of no more than four elements.
- Tell a story that helps the audience to organize the parts.
- Provide concrete, specific evidence to support your conclusions.
- Prepare an outline for each part that has two or more subparts.
- Conclude each part and subpart with a summary.
- Consider marking your progress with a banner or other signpost.
- Build in breaks that allow the audience to "come up for air"; give the audience time to digest what you've said.
- Repeat the opening outline at the end, to remind the audience what the presentation was about.
- Prepare text and graphics to emphasize your final conclusions.
- Set up a snappy ending.
- Don't rush it: Don't talk so fast that the audience members are still straining to understand one sentence as you are saying the next, and don't whip through the slides so fast that the audience can't take them in.
- Read the most important material aloud because it will give you the advantage of providing two ways—visual and verbal—for the audience to store what you have to say.

Legible Text

3

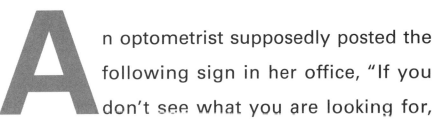

An optometrist supposedly posted the following sign in her office, "If you don't see what you are looking for, you've come to the right place." But not being able to read text easily in a PowerPoint presentation is no laughing matter; in fact, it might give the audience the opposite sign, that they've come to the wrong place.

Virtually all presentations include text, and illegible text is a major cause of many confusing PowerPoint presentations. In this chapter you'll find recommendations for how to create clear and legible bulleted lists, labels, titles, tables, and keys.

Let's start with the most basic element of all: what font you use for your text.

Ten Tips on Fonts

To use the immortal words of President George W. Bush, "If we don't succeed, we run the risk of failure." There is no easier way to fail than to ensure that the audience cannot read the words on your slides. In this section, I present recommendations to how to avoid the risk of failure because the audience sees only smudges instead of words, or has to strain to decode your text. Here we will focus on fonts. The term "font" refers here to the general appearance of letters; fonts vary in terms of their typeface (such as Times or Ariel), style (such as *italics*, UPPERCASE, or **bold** vs. normal weight), size, and color. Many fonts are available for the PowerPoint program, and to some degree your choice will be dictated by your personal taste. However, some fonts are definitely better than others for presentations.

1.   Avoid all uppercase, all italics, or all bold.

Fonts in which letters share many features are difficult to read because it is not easy to separate one letter from the next, so the viewer must look carefully at each letter.

Example: compare abcdefghijklmnop versus ABCDEFGHI-JKLMNOP. The forms of the letters in the second font are more similar than in the first.

- Use mixed uppercase and lowercase letters; don't use all uppercase letters, which are much more alike than a mixture of upper- and lowercase letters (and also, who wants to be shouted at?).
- Use standard font whenever possible; don't use italics for more than a word or two.
- Use normal weight as the default, and don't use bold throughout; letters in bold are less discriminable than normal weight letters, and also are too salient.

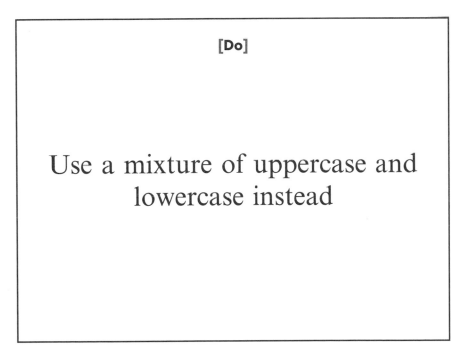

[Don't]

DON'T USE ALL UPPERCASE
and don't use all italics

[Do]

Use a mixture of uppercase and lowercase instead

2.   **Don't underline.**

Underlining cuts off the bottoms of letters that have descending lines (such as p and g), which makes them harder to identify. If you want to emphasize a word, put it in italics (provided that the letters are still easy to distinguish in that font), make it bold, or use a more salient color.

[Don't]

Don't underline

[Do]

Use **bold,** *italics,* or a change in color for emphasis

---

3. **Use different colors only for emphasis or to specify different classes of information.**

> You're likely to notice the nail that sticks up above the boards because attention is drawn to large differences. Like that nail, changes in color draw attention, and we expect changes in color to

signal changes in content. So don't change the color of the font unless you want to emphasize something or distinguish among different classes of information. (For color versions of the examples below, see insert, Figures 3.3a and 3.3b.)

- When using color to signal a change, use a color for only one term or phrase. If you make more than one word the same color, know

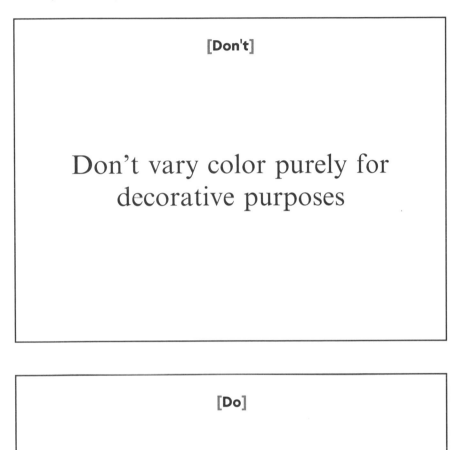

that readers will tend to group together words in the same color—even if you are only using the color for emphasis and the words are not in fact closely related.

- Avoid using more than three different colors; too many colors can easily produce too many perceptual units and overwhelm the viewers' short-term memory capacity.

4. Use different fonts only for emphasis or to specify different classes of information.

Vary the font only to emphasize or group material into distinct classes.

5. Use fonts that are easy to read.

Editorial style manuals often urge us not to use a twenty-five-cent word when an easier-to-understand nickel one will do. The simpler-is-better rule also goes for fonts. At first blush, you might think that a fancy font will make you look sophisticated. Not so. You may see the font as fancy, but the audience may see it as an obstruction. Instead of making you look good, an ornate font will make the

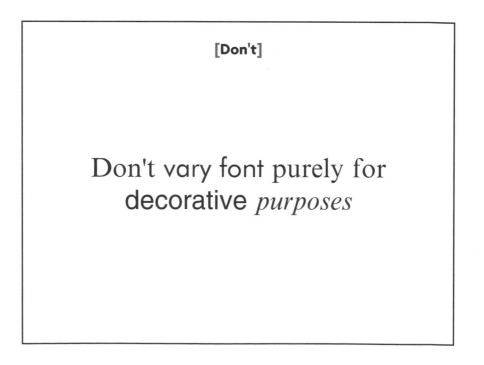

[Do]

Vary font only for *emphasis* or to group words together

---

audience work harder. Letters in such fonts take more time and energy to read because the viewer must search for the relevant lines and try to shut out the flourishes. Even worse, such letters may also clump together visually, making the words difficult to distinguish.

[Don't]

Don't use visually complex fonts

[Do]

Use visually simple fonts

---

6.   Ensure that words are large enough to read easily.

Text must be clearly discernible even to the viewers sitting at the very back of the room. To get a sense of their viewpoint, stand about three feet from your computer screen. If you can read the text on it without effort, it's probably large enough for your presentation. But the key is not the actual size of the letters on your computer screen—or even their size measured on the screen during a presentation. Instead, the key is the visual extent of the letters, as seen from a specific distance: As you move farther from the screen, the letters occupy an increasingly smaller visual extent (think of taking a photo of the screen from different distances—the size of the text in the photo will be increasingly smaller as you move increasingly far from the screen). More precisely, hold up your thumb at arm's length and look at it through one eye. The optimal size for letters is a bit less than one-quarter of the visual extent of your thumb as it appears at arm's length.

7.   Ensure that viewers can easily discriminate text from the background.

The PowerPoint program lets you use many dramatic and interesting background patterns. But before becoming too enamored with those celestial scenes or dramatic splashes of color, check to make sure that the background isn't so salient, or (worse) similar to the text, that it's difficult to read the information-conveying words.

[Don't]

Ensure that the font is large enough to be seen from the back of the room

[Do]

Ensure that the font is large enough to be seen from the back of the room

- If you want to use such backgrounds, lower their contrast to make them, well, "fade into the background," letting your text assert itself in the foreground (see Figure 3.7b).
- To be on the safe side, use a background with low contrast and an even color, and a font color that is easily discriminated.

Example: An orange-yellow or gold font on a dark gray background is highly discriminable, as is a white font on any highly saturated "cool" color, or a black font on a very unsaturated, pale color. (See Chapter 4 for more detail.)

8. Use either a serif or sans serif font, but don't mix and mingle them arbitrarily.

Typefaces are divided into two general classes, *serif* and *sans serif*. Serif typefaces (such as Times and Palatino) have little feet, brackets and hooks at the ends of the lines used in the letters; sans serif typefaces (such as Ariel and Century Gothic) have only straightforward strokes. Use the same font consistently—otherwise changes will be taken to convey information, and **the** text may *look* `very strange` and is harder to read.

Figure 3.7a. If the background is too salient, viewers will have to work to discriminate text from the background. A display should not be a haystack, with your message the needle. If you use a patterned background, make sure that it does not bury the text and that it is not so salient as to distract from your message. (See color version in insert.)

Figure 3.7b. (For color version, see insert.)

- If fonts are so small that they are barely legible, then sans serif is better because in a serif font, the little feet, brackets, and hooks in different letters become inappropriately grouped together, making the letters hard to distinguish.
- If the contrast or luminance (which our perceptual systems register as brightness) is so low that viewers can barely see the type, then serif fonts are better because the aforementioned little feet, brackets, and hooks provide additional cues regarding the identity of each letter.

That said, if these variables are important, reconsider your slides! You should never put the audience in the position of having to read words that are too small or hard to see! The bottom line: If you present text at a large enough size and in conditions of sufficient contrast and illumination, then any standard (such as Ariel or Times, not ornate or "fancy") typeface is acceptable.

9. Use standard fonts.

Unfortunately, fonts do not always appear the same when you make your actual presentation as they did on your computer screen. Not all

---

[Don't]

If fonts are very small, so that they are barely legible, use sans serif font; if the contrast or luminance is low, so that fonts that should be visible can barely be seen, use serif fonts.

[Do]

If the font is large enough and visible enough, either serif or sans serif font is acceptable

---

computers are loaded with the same font set, and some projectors have low resolution, which can also lead to illegible type. To be safe, use serif fonts such as Times New Roman (the most common), Garamond, or Century Schoolbook, or sans serif fonts such as Arial, Verdana, or Tahoma. I used to use only Palatino on the Mac, but I discovered that some computers don't have this font and will substitute Times New Roman, which changes the presentation's spacing. Printers will also substitute for fonts they don't recognize, so don't count on your printouts looking the same if you use an uncommon font. To be on the safe side, use TrueType™ fonts, and an XGA (1024 × 768 resolution) projector. To quote President Bush again, "One word sums up properly the responsibility of any governor, and that one word is 'to be prepared.' "

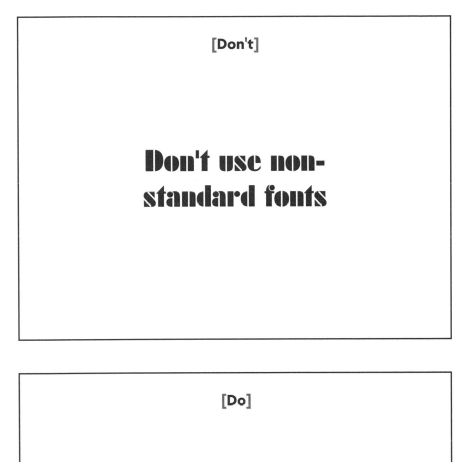

[Don't]

Don't use non-standard fonts

[Do]

Use standard fonts

10.   **Ensure that only the relevant words are distinguishable from the background.**

I recently watched a DVD of a concert by the rock band the Who. Fourteen musicians were on stage, but the spotlights picked out only the three (then) surviving members of the original band. Without the spotlights, it would have been easy to be distracted by the new lead guitar player, or that attractive woman singing backups. You need to supply the spotlight for your audience, leading them to pay attention to just the part of the slide that's immediately relevant. To ensure that the audience members' attention will not wander, gray out all parts of the slide but the section you are discussing (see Figure 3.10b). As noted earlier, by "gray out," I mean switch the color or density so that the font is just barely distinguishable from the background. When you gray out an irrelevant part of your presentation, the viewer will be aware that something is there, but not be tempted to attend to it. Present each new section when it becomes relevant by changing its contrast to the background.

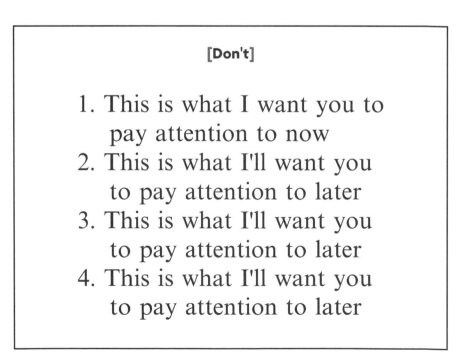

Figure 3.10a. Use graying out to direct the audience's attention to what is relevant at a particular point in the presentation.

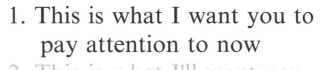

[Do]

1. This is what I want you to pay attention to now
2. This is what I'll want you to pay attention to later
3. This is what I'll want you to pay attention to later
4. This is what I'll want you to pay attention to later

Figure 3.10b.

Bullets: Guidelines for Straight Shooting

Bullets are a convenient way to present the separate elements of a list. However, bullets are a bit like salt—often essential to bring out the best, but distasteful if overdone.

1. Present a quick overview of a list, then gray out all but the first entry.

Begin by presenting a complete list of bulleted items, but only long enough for the viewers to see the length of the list. Ensure that the audience pays attention only to the first item on your list (which will be salient) by graying out everything but this item, so that the remainder of the list can be seen, but not easily read.

2. Present items individually, highlighting only one at a time as you go from top to bottom.

Finish reading and discussing each item before you present the next. Gray out all entries other than the one you are presenting, including the previous one, which will ensure that you direct the viewers' attention to just the material you want them to focus on.

3. Use bullets only for topic sentences or specific cases.

Bulleted entries on a list should provide only key concepts or examples. Don't present every word in your entire presentation in bulleted lists: Present no more and no less than you need to help the viewers organize and understand your message.

Example: Present only enough information in an opening outline to orient the viewers (the panel shown below, Figure 3.11a, would be overwhelming, even in the best of circumstances).

4. Give the audience time to read each bulleted item.

Don't be caught saying one thing while the audience is trying to read another.

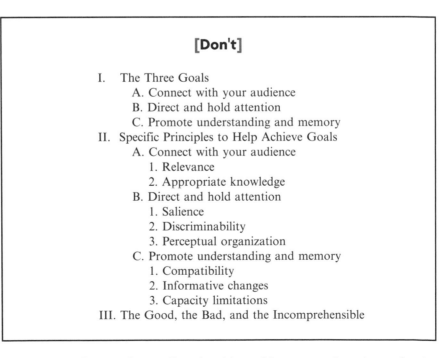

Figure 3.11a. An opening outline should provide a general road map for the presentation. The material above is not only overwhelming, but much of it won't mean anything to the audience until they've heard later parts of the presentation.

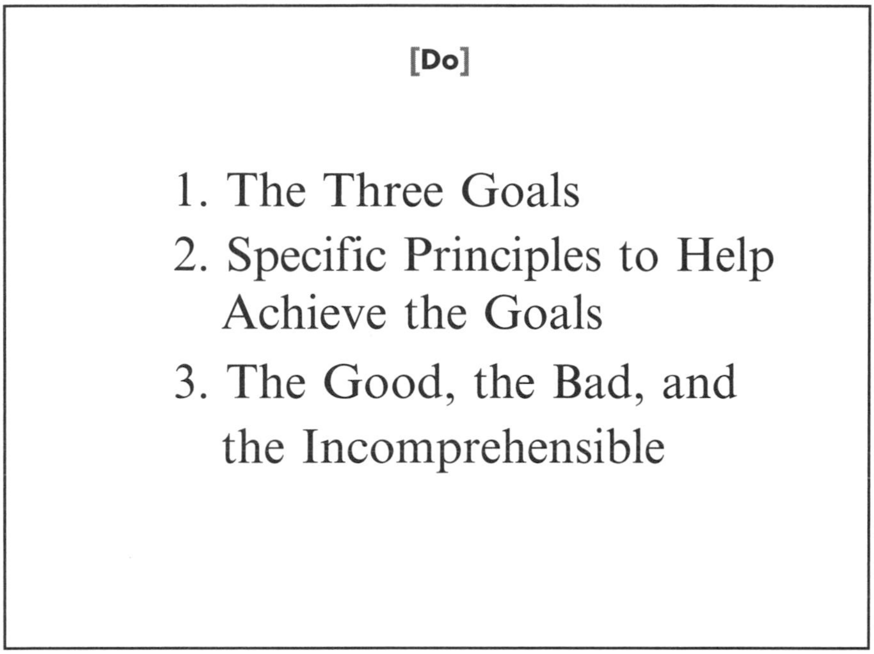

[Do]

1. The Three Goals
2. Specific Principles to Help Achieve the Goals
3. The Good, the Bad, and the Incomprehensible

Figure 3.11b.

5. Discuss only material closely related to the current entry.

After you read a bulleted item, you can expand on the concept, such as by paraphrasing it or providing an anecdote that illustrates it. But stay close to that concept. If you present a new idea, use another bullet. In general, discuss only material that is closely related to what is currently being shown on a slide.

6. Use no more than two lines per bulleted entry.

As a general rule, include no more than two lines per entry in a bulleted list. Two lines are roughly enough space for four concepts, which—as codified in our *Rule of Four*—is all that viewers can reflect on easily at any one time. A concept corresponds to a word or phrase that expresses an idea. A simple rule of thumb for identifying the number of concepts is to count the nouns and verbs. For example, "Use two lines per bulleted entry" includes three concepts: "Use," "lines," and "entry." (In fact, concepts usually can be decomposed into groups of concepts, such as "two lines" and "bulleted entry" — but these combinations serve as single groups, which is all that is important for present purposes.)

[Don't]

This presentation will focus on the psychological principles that make a PowerPoint presentation clear and persuasive and will explain how to use those principles to improve your presentations

---

[Do]

Principles for making compelling PowerPoint presentations

Figure 3.12. As a general rule, two lines is about right for each bulleted entry. Try reading aloud the one on the top; if it's a mouthful for you, it's an earful for the audience.

7. Respect the *Rule of Four*: Use hierarchical organization, with no more than four items at each level.

If you have more than four concepts or items to present, organize them into categories and present each category in a separate slide. If you do this, first present a slide in which you list the categories in the order in which they will be presented, which will prepare the audience for what is to come.

Example: If you want to list 20 types of items commonly found in convenience stores, figure out how to organize them into four or fewer categories, then divide each category into four or fewer categories. As shown in Figure 3.13b, you might make an initial cut between food items and sundries (with perhaps 12 food items and 8 sundries); you then could divide the food items into four categories (such as candy, vegetables, baked goods, and dairy products) and the sundries into two categories.

[Don't]

Socks
Twix
Snickers
Sunglasses
Mars bars
Caps
Carrots
Peas
Squash
Insect repellant
Shoe laces
Shampoo
Bread
Hand lotion
Hotdog buns
Cake
Chap Stick
Donuts
Milk
Ice cream

Figure 3.13a. If you must present every single item, organize them into categories, each of which should contain no more than four entries. But before doing this, think again: Does the audience really need to see every one of those individual items? Would selected examples help you to make your point more clearly?

[Do]

Food Items	Sundries
Candy	*Wearables*
Twix	Sunglasses
Snickers	Socks
Mars bars	Shoe laces
	Caps
Vegetables	
Carrots	*Consumables*
Peas	Hand lotion
Squash	Chap Stick
	Insect repellant
Baked goods	Shampoo
Bread	
Hotdog buns	
Cake	
Donuts	
Diary	
Milk	
Ice cream	

Figure 3.13b.

However, this advice is based on the assumption that each item is in fact important to the point you are making. If the individual items are not important (for instance, it could have been bagels instead of donuts), then all you need to do is present the categories and perhaps list selected examples of the items. Present no more and no less than the audience actually needs to know.

8.   Use the same bullet symbol for each entry in a slide.

The standard "●" bullet is tried and true, and a wide range of viewers will have no problem understanding what it signifies. So as a general rule, you will not go wrong using the standard bullet symbol. But you can use another symbol for a bullet if you are certain that the audience will understand it, and that the symbol has special relevance to your presentation.

Example: A small dollar sign might be appropriate if you are listing sources of income.

- Don't change the shape of the bullets in your presentation unless you want to signal a change in category. Viewers will assume that any visual change—replacing round bullets with arrows, for example—is intended to highlight something new about the material you are presenting.

• However, if you do use different symbols for bullets for different classes of information (e.g., income, number of workers, amount of rainfall in different locations), keep in mind that the audience will need a moment to understand that the different symbols function as bullets.

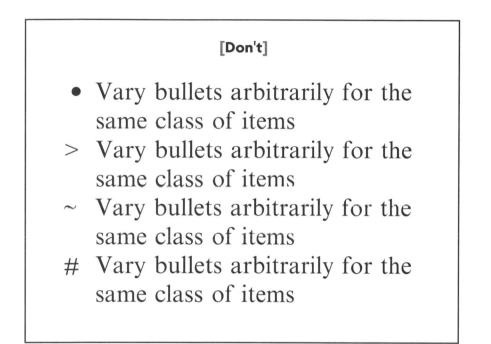

[Don't]

- Vary bullets arbitrarily for the same class of items
> Vary bullets arbitrarily for the same class of items
~ Vary bullets arbitrarily for the same class of items
# Vary bullets arbitrarily for the same class of items

[Do]

- Use the same bullet for the same classes of items
- Don't change the shape of bullets arbitrarily
- Use a standard bullet unless there's a good reason not to
- If you use a novel bullet, ensure that it is appropriate

Always remember that your job is to communicate clearly and compellingly, keeping the audience's attention throughout your presentation; so consider whether it's worth including additional features that will require the audience to work harder. As a general rule, my advice is to avoid taxing the audience's natural limitations if at all possible, particularly with formatting.

Labels: Guidelines for Making Words and Objects Work Together

In many cases you will pair words with graphics or tables, such as charts, graphs, diagrams, or illustrations (including photographs). Some labels are easier to grasp than others, and some may be effective only if the viewers are engaged and thinking through the implications of what you say. Consider this (probably apocryphal story): A member of the Massachusetts Senate, which has sometimes been a site of high drama and strong words, lost his temper after watching his colleagues vote for an obvious piece of Pure Pork, and, pounding on his desk, shouted, "Half of this Senate is made up of idiots and corrupt politicians!" The chamber broke into an angry babble, and the Senators demanded that he retract this slander. Looking up toward the ceiling, as if beseeching divine guidance, the offending senator spoke in a softer voice: "I retract my previous statement. Half of this august body is NOT made up of idiots and corrupt politicians!" The first statement required no work to grasp its meaning, and the second one is (moderately) amusing because it is clear only after you put a tiny bit of work into decoding its implications. (I've heard this one in various forms, and adapted this version from http://jokes.comedycentral.com—which, in spite of the source, is no joke.) But if the audience is distracted or otherwise not motivated to pay attention, they may not draw out even simple implications. Don't risk it; serve up your offering as transparently and directly as possible.

1.   Use terms that convey the appropriate denotations and connotations.

Words not only have *denotations* (direct meanings) but also *connotations* (indirect meanings), and you need to make sure that both are appropriate for your particular audience and for the point you want to make.

Example: You could describe a new idea as "innovative" (which has a positive connotation) or "new-fangled" (which has a negative connotation). If you are promoting the idea, the connotation of the second term would get in your way.

2.   Label every graphic, table, and their information-bearing parts—unless the identity is self-evident.

No matter how fascinating you and your material may be, some members of the audience may allow their attention to wander from time to time. In fact, if your presentation is unusually stimulating, you may be rewarded by sparking the audience to consider implications and applications—which will inadvertently result in their missing snatches of what you have to say. As a general rule, label everything important, so that viewers can read what they failed to hear.

Example: If you have a photo of a historical personage, provide the name; if you have a map of Beijing, label it.

- Don't label symbols or material that are extremely familiar to the audience, such as a picture of the current president or a very famous landmark. If information is not needed, don't supply it (if you do, the audience might think that you are talking down to them).

3.   Group labels with the appropriate elements of the display.

To ensure that each label is clearly associated with the element it identifies, keep in mind the various aspects of the Principle of Perceptual Organization, and beware of the following:

- Viewers will group labels that are placed near a graphic with that graphic; so place labels only near graphics to which they apply.
- Viewers will see labels that seem to flow from the end of a line as part of that line, and hence assume that the labels apply to that line. Avoid this arrangement unless the label does in fact apply.
- Viewers will group labels that are the same color as an element with that element (e.g., green labels with green wedges, blue labels with blue wedges, and so forth). Such grouping is confusing when the labels don't in fact apply to the elements with the same color, so avoid doing this.

4.   **Label content elements directly.**

Place labels immediately next to or within the corresponding content elements, such as objects, bars, lines, or wedges of a pie chart. If it is not possible to place a label near what it identifies, or if placing such a label creates clutter, use a key. But use a key only as a last resort because a key will force the audience to memorize and search, and both tasks require effort that the audience may not be willing to expend.

5.   **Make words in the same label close together and typographically similar.**

Take advantage of the Principle of Perceptual Organization by ensuring that words in the same label do cohere as a unit and don't group individually with other parts of the display.

- Place the letters, numbers, and words in a label relatively close to one another.
- Make the letters, numbers, and words in a label the same size, color, and brightness.
- Be certain that labels are not so close to one another that they group together improperly.

   Example: These words group properly . . . These words . . . do . . . NOT.

6.   **Use more salient labels to identify more important parts of the display.**

As we know from the Principle of Salience, our visual systems reflexively attend to extreme values and large differences in line length and width, shading, color, motion, and other visual properties. As a result, we notice heavier lines before thinner ones, lines that contrast with the color of their backgrounds before lines that blend with their backgrounds, brighter colors before dimmer ones, thicker bars before thinner ones, and moving objects before stationary ones. In accordance with the Principle of Salience, we should

- make the labels for the most important parts of the display more salient (for example, by having them be relatively large, bold, a striking color, or moving in from the side).
- make the labels for increasingly smaller details, or more fine-grained components, decreasingly less salient.

7.   **Use hierarchical labeling.**

Take a look at the two panels, labeled "Don't" and "Do" in the illustration below. Did Hillsborough or Pinellas have greater sales of single-family homes in 1991? This is relatively easy to determine from Do, but much harder from Don't. When the label refers to two or more dimensions, use a hierarchical labeling system. A hierarchical labeling system is one in which some labels apply to groups of other labels; the "higher in the hierarchy" the label is, the larger it should be. As illustrated in Figure 3.15b, "Do," using a hierarchical labeling system achieves three goals. This scheme

- eliminates the need for a key, which taxes the processing capacities of the audience members because it requires them to search for the corresponding parts of the display;
- specifies each of the relevant dimensions separately, which helps the audience to make specific comparisons;
- removes redundant labels, which clutter a display, thereby making it more difficult to pick out the other elements.

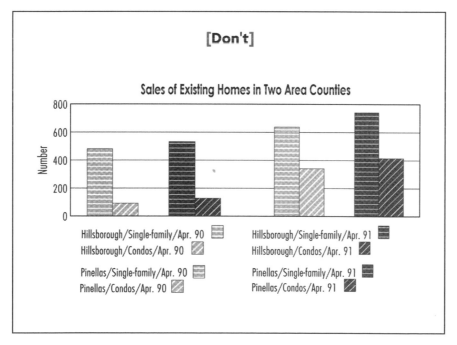

Figure 3.15a.

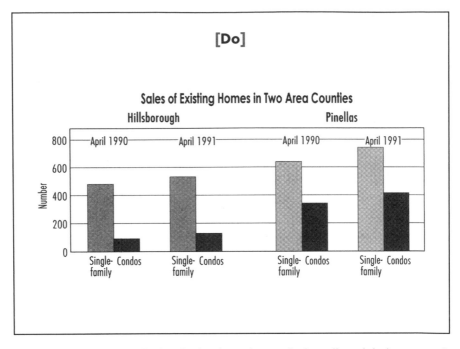

Figure 3.15b. Not only is the display less cluttered when direct labels are used, but also the bars are easier to compare along specific dimensions (dwelling type, county, year) when the labels specify the dimensions separately.

8. Use the same size and font for labels that identify the same types of components.

When we see a difference, we expect it to mean something and are confused if it doesn't. Labels for each of the same type of component (wedges, bars, etc.) should use the same font and be the same size. Entities of equal importance should be labeled with the same font and be the same size.

Example: If you have two pictures of former CEOs and the sizes of their names or their photos are different, the audience will draw the obvious conclusion about your level of regard for each.

9. Use the same terminology in labels, as well as in the surrounding text and spoken words.

Using different terms in a display, in text, and in what you say aloud may lead the audience to wonder if you mean different things. Attempting to distinguish these differences will definitely tax the cognitive capacities of your audience.

Example: Don't label birds "birds" on a slide while referring to "fowl" in text or in your spoken remarks.

Titles: 4 Simple Guidelines

The psychological principles will also help you to create titles for your slides.

1. Title a slide to focus attention on the most important information.

I recently ran across the following quote, attributed to the late Jerry Garcia (of the Grateful Dead rock band): "I read somewhere that 77 percent of all the mentally ill live in poverty. Actually, I'm more intrigued by the 23 percent who are apparently doing quite well for themselves." He was right! To convey a different message, someone could have said, "Twenty-three percent of the mentally ill do well financially." Until I read Mr. Garcia's remark, I hadn't ever looked at it that way. In general, the same information can be presented in many different ways; different aspects can be highlighted over other aspects. You need to decide what's the conceptual foreground and what's the conceptual background. The title of a slide tells the reader what is the foreground (and, if relevant, what is the background).

- When formulating a title, ask yourself: What material do you want to stress? Does it apply in particular to a specific time (year, month) and place (country, region of a state)?
- Include only the most relevant information in the title. Define the foreground, and only mention the background if it is immediately relevant.
- Mention what's most important first.

Example: "Effects of mental illness on earnings of men versus women" puts "mental illness" in the foreground and gender in the background, whereas "Effects of gender on earnings in the mentally ill" puts gender in the foreground and mental illness in the background.

2. Make the title typographically distinct.

The title should be the most salient element of the display. Use the most salient font for the title, to catch the eye immediately.

3. Present the title of a complex slide before the content elements are clearly visible.

Leading with the title will force your audience to pay attention to it, which will give them a framework for understanding the rest of your material more easily. So, if you have a very elaborate slide, present the title first, with everything else grayed out (i.e., in a very low-contrast font).

4. Center the title at the top of the slide.

Audiences are used to seeing titles at the tops of documents, so that is where they expect the title to be on your slides. If it is off center, the audience may group it with one part of the slide, rather than with the whole slide.

If you place the title anywhere but the center of the top—for example, in the left margin—you must follow this convention through your entire presentation, creating a distinctive but consistent design. Viewers will grow familiar with this design and will quickly come to group the title properly. However, an unconventional style will initially make viewers work harder than a conventional one will.

Tables: 8 Legs to Stand On

Tables include lists of numbers or words organized into rows and columns. Here are eight recommendations that will help you make your tables more useful.

1. Use a table of numbers only when specific values are important.

Use a table of numbers only if it is important to convey specific values, as opposed to differences among values. You will be better off using a graph if your goal is simply to show that one entity is greater than another.

2. Don't use a table if trends or interactions are important.

If your goal is to present a specific trend (such as increased revenues over time) or a difference between trends (such as increased revenues over time in one part of the world with no such increases in another), use a line graph. Using a table would force viewers to compute and compare differences among differences of numbers, which requires work. As always, don't make viewers struggle to grasp your message.

3. Show complex tables to emphasize that the data are complex or to show a data point in context.

Just as Abe Lincoln would never have been silly enough to try to use a PowerPoint presentation to deliver the Gettysburg address, you should not even think of using such a presentation as a substitute for a research article. PowerPoint presentations and research articles just aren't the same things; they have different purposes. In an article, you need to report all the details (and thus a complex table is appropriate). In a presentation, you need to show how material leads to a certain conclusion and shouldn't ask viewers to spend even 5 minutes sitting silently in their seats, pondering the various differences among numbers in a table you project.

The only time to present a very complex table is when you want to make the point that

- there are a lot of data arranged in orderly ways, or
- to highlight a single value (e.g., by putting it in red) and show it in relation to the table as a whole. In this case, consider including a follow-on slide in which you "zoom in" on the critical value and its immediate surrounds.

If you have so many entries that they must be very small in order to fit on a slide, this is a painfully clear signal that your table is not going to be very useful for other purposes. You will probably be better off splitting the table into two or more slides. If this won't work, consider using a bar graph to present averages (with some measure of variation, such as the standard error of the mean, around each average value) rather than a table.

4. Present only the information needed to make your point.

A friend of mine sent me an e-mail about the following incident (I'm not sure whether this was supposed to be accurate or a joke, but either way it makes my point): A high school chemistry teacher was annoyed at her class for not mastering the Periodic Table; the students didn't seem to understand why the table is important and hadn't put much effort into memorizing it by rote. In a mild pique, the teacher told her students that when she was their age, she knew all the elements in the table backward and forward. One soft voice from the back of the room muttered in reply, "Sure, but in those days there were only a few to learn." She couldn't help but smile, but if you show a very complex table without providing a very good reason for it, your audience probably won't. Present no more information than you need to make your point (and no less). Keep in mind that unnecessary distinctions can confuse the audience just as quickly as unnecessary data.

Example: If you are not interested in monthly fluctuations, don't present values broken down by month.

5. Organize a table to emphasize more important distinctions.

Use formatting to emphasize the most important aspects of the presented information.

Example: If you are presenting data from men and women in two countries, and the gender difference is more important for your point, you would organize the table as on the left of Table 3.1. If, on the other hand, country is more important, then you would organize the data as on the right. Note again the use of hierarchical labeling.

Table 3.1

	Men		Women			USA		Canada	
	USA	Canada	USA	Canada		Men	Women	Men	Women
Measure 1	14	15	12	10	Measure 1	14	12	15	10
Measure 2	10	18	9	10	Measure 2	10	9	18	10
Measure 3	12	14	14	13	Measure 3	12	14	14	13
Measure 4	10	12	10	12	Measure 4	10	10	12	12

6. In complex tables, include summary statistics and make them salient.

If you need to present more than two columns and two rows of numbers, include summary statistics (e.g., means or sums, as appropriate for your message) at the bottoms of the columns and right-hand sides of the rows. (In the trade, these summary statistics are known as "marginal values.")

- Summary statistics should be heavier, larger, or more salient in some other way (e.g., having a brighter color) than the entries in the table.

7. In complex tables, include grid lines.

If you need to present more than two columns and two rows, use grid lines. Grid lines will not only help viewers to organize the table but will also guide their eyes from the labels of rows and columns to the specific entries.

8. If the entries are labeled with pictures or icons, ensure that they evoke the appropriate concept.

People are more likely to name objects consistently if a picture illustrates a "prototypical example" (i.e., an average member) of the category. If you want to use graphics to label entries in a table, ensure that the audience will easily associate the graphics with the appropriate entities.

Example: If you want to illustrate different kinds of animals that are kept as pets, an average-looking mutt is more likely to be labeled "dog" than a St. Bernard would be.

The Key: Factors That Make It Work

A key has two components: (1) patches of a graphic or table that correspond to individual components; and (2) labels that identify these patches. These patches typically consist of squares that contain different colors, texture patterns, or segments of dashed versus solid lines.

1. Use a key when direct labels cannot be used.

A key requires the viewer to memorize an association between labels and portions of the graphic or table, and then to find those portions in order to identify them. So you should avoid using a key unless absolutely necessary. There are two exceptions to this recommendation, both of which are illustrated in Figure 3.16, "Do":

- Use a key when there are so many wedges, objects, or segments in a small space that is impossible to label them directly because the labels would not group properly or they would have to be so small as to be illegible.
- Use a key when the same entities appear in more than two parts of a graphic or table, so a key will reduce clutter and the difficulty of searching for labels.

That said, if you need a key, consider whether you want to show the graphic or table in your presentation; the display may simply be too complicated to be grasped easily in this context. If you do need it:

- consider building up the display a part at a time, so that the key becomes a way to keep track of the separate parts you have shown.
- be sure to point out explicitly the relation between parts of the key and the corresponding parts of the display.

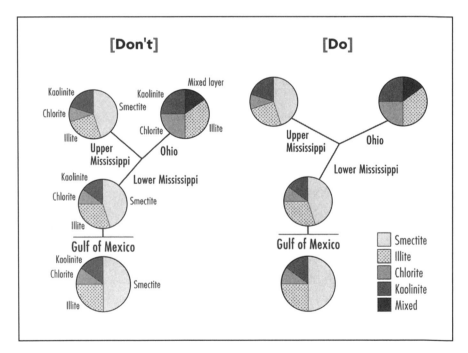

Figure 3.16. A key is sometimes appropriate, particularly when it reduces clutter and allows the structure of the display itself to be more prominent.

2.   Place a key at the top right of a single panel or centered over multiple panels.

In a single-panel display, the key is by convention positioned at the top right; in a multipanel display, which contains more than one variant of the same graphic (such as graphs or diagrams), it is centered at the top, directly beneath the title. Viewers familiar with graphics will expect to find the key in one of these locations. If aesthetic or other considerations lead you to put the key in an unconventional location (such as in the example you just saw), realize that the viewers may have to search for it, which will tax their limited processing capacity. However, if you consistently place the key in the same location in a number of displays, the viewers will soon learn where to find it.

3.   Ensure that labels and patches are easy to tell apart.

Ensure that each label and patch in the key is discriminable from the back of the room and when the lights are turned on. To ensure that they are discriminable, you may need to make patches larger than they would be if you were publishing the display in an article. Furthermore, if you use different textures in the patches and in the corresponding portions of the display, keep in mind that a Power-Point slide does not have the resolution of a published figure (and thus relatively coarse patterns are appropriate for PowerPoint).

In addition, if you want the audience to make specific comparisons, it's a good idea to point out explicitly the correspondence between the relevant patches in the key and the portion or portions of the display they label.

4.   Ensure that corresponding labels and patches form perceptual groups.

Associate the label and the patch by making sure that they are closer to each other than to any other part of the key; the proximity will then group the elements properly.

5.   Use the same order for patches and their corresponding content elements.

The patches in the key should be presented in the same order as the corresponding content elements (bars, icons, etc.) in the display itself.

Example: If the labeled patches in the key refer to elements in a row, as in "Do," the top element should refer to the leftmost content element in the display, the second from the top element should refer to the content element second from the left, and so forth. These guidelines are followed in "Do" of Figure 3.17.

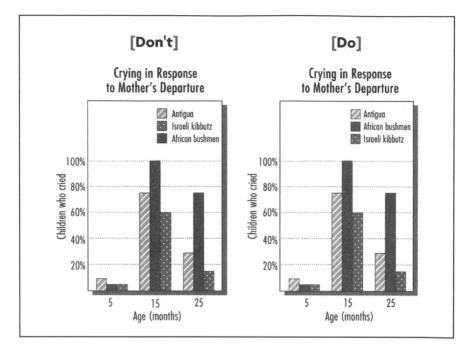

Figure 3.17. Viewers will have to search for corresponding bars if the order of the key does not match the order of the content elements.

From the Principles to the Point

These recommendations are based on the same psychological principles discussed earlier. Let's revisit them and note which ones contributed the most to each of the major recommendations I offer.

Principle of Relevance: Communication is most effective when neither too much nor too little information is presented. (We understand and remember a message more easily when the right amount of detail is used to make the point.)

- Present a quick overview of a list, then gray out all but the first entry.
- Ensure that only the relevant words are easily distinguishable from the background.
- Present items individually, highlighting only one at a time as you go from top to bottom.
- Use bullets only for topic sentences or specific cases.
- Title a slide to focus attention on the most important information.
- Use a table of numbers only when specific values are important.
- Present only the information needed to make your point.

Principle of Appropriate Knowledge: Communication requires prior knowledge of pertinent concepts, jargon, and symbols. (We understand and remember a message more easily if it connects to what we already know.)

- Use standard fonts.
- Use terms that convey the appropriate denotations and connotations for your audience and the point you want to make.
- Center the title at the top of the slide.
- Place a key at the top right of a single panel or centered over multiple panels.

Principle of Salience: Attention is drawn to large perceptible differences. (Big relative differences grab attention.)

- Use more salient labels to label more important components of the display, and use less salient labels for details or smaller components.
- Make the title typographically distinct.

Principle of Discriminability: Two properties must differ by a large enough proportion or they will not be distinguished. (We need contrast to distinguish shapes, colors, or positions from each other and from the background.)

- Avoid all uppercase, all italic, or all bold typefaces.
- Don't underline (use bold, color, or italics for emphasis).
- Use fonts that are easy to read.
- Use visually simple fonts.
- Ensure that words are large enough to be read easily.
- Ensure that viewers can easily discriminate text from the background.
- Use either a serif or a sans serif font, but do not mix and mingle them arbitrarily.
- If entries in a table are too small to be read, show the table in two or more slides.
- Ensure that labels and patches are easy to tell apart.

Principle of Perceptual Organization: People automatically group elements into units, which they then attend to and remember. (These groups are easier to see and remember than the isolated components would be.)

- Group labels with the appropriate elements of the display.
- Label content elements directly whenever space permits.
- Make words in the same label close together and typographically similar.
- In complex tables, include grid lines.

- Organize a table to emphasize more important distinctions.
- Ensure that corresponding labels and patches form perceptual groups.

Principle of Compatibility: A message is easiest to understand if its form is compatible with its meaning. (For better or worse, the mind tends to judge a book by its cover.)

- If entries are labeled with pictures or icons, ensure that they evoke the appropriate concept.
- Discuss only material that is closely related to what is currently being shown on a slide.
- Don't use a table if trends or interactions are important (usually, use a line graph).

Principle of Informative Changes: People expect changes in properties to carry information. (And we expect every necessary piece of information to be indicated by a change in a perceptible property.)

- Use different colors only for emphasis or to specify different classes of information.
- Use different fonts only for emphasis or to specify different classes of information.
- Use the same bullet symbol for each entry in a list of similar items; change bullet symbols only to indicate a change in the nature of the entry.
- Label every graphic, table, and their information-bearing parts— unless the identity is self-evident.
- Use the same size and font for labels that identify the same types of components.
- Use the same terminology in labels as well as in the surrounding text and spoken words.
- Use the same order for patches in a key and their corresponding content elements in a graphic or table.

Principle of Capacity Limitations: People have a limited capacity to retain and to process information, and so will not understand a message if too much information must be retained or processed. (From a communicative point of view, less can be more!)

- Present parts of complex displays individually, growing the whole from the parts.
- Give the audience time to read each bulleted item.
- Use no more than two lines per bulleted entry.
- Show no more than four bulleted items in a single list.

- Respect the *Rule of Four*: Use hierarchical organization, with no more than four items at each level.
- Use hierarchical labeling.
- Present the title of a complex slide before the easily visible content elements.
- Show complex tables to emphasize that the data are complex or to show a data point in context.
- In complex tables, include summary statistics and make them salient.
- Use a key when direct labels cannot be used.

If you master the principles, you won't need to memorize every one of the recommendations any more than you need to memorize every sentence you might say today. Just as you can generate sentences on the basis of your (unconscious) knowledge of grammar and words, with practice you can learn to generate good PowerPoint presentations on the basis of your knowledge of human mental processes.

Color, Texture, Animation, and Sound

4

Our ability to sense color has adaptive value. For example, it helps us know when fruit is ripe. It's a fact that people who have lost the ability to see color (following brain damage) report that their perception of food has changed dramatically (for example, one such person described a tomato as "black and repulsive").

In general, color helps us notice what's different and what's the same; we easily see clusters of ripe red apples against the green of the tree's leaves, or a red sign mounted on a black wall. These functions of color perception in everyday life don't go away when we see PowerPoint presentations; vision operates the same way—for better or worse—regardless of whether we are viewing apple trees or PowerPoint slides.

In addition to color, almost all information graphics software uses textures as filling (both in the foreground and the background), and many PowerPoint presentations use animation (i.e., movements on the screen) and sound—both within a slide and in transitions between slides. Again, the cognitive mechanisms that pick up and process such information during everyday life don't go away when we attend a PowerPoint presentation; they operate the same way, which can either help or hurt the presentation. In this chapter I summarize recommendations for using color, texture, animation, and sound.

Color: The 12 Essentials

Color not only adds visual interest to a display but also can help you to communicate effectively. If used improperly, however, variations in color can obscure your message. To help you understand how to use color to make your presentations eye-catching and compelling, I first need to explain some essential facts about color. If you understand why I make my recommendations, you won't need to memorize them.

Color is composed of three distinct aspects:

1. Light can be thought of as a series of waves, similar to regularly spaced waves on the surface of the ocean. The longer the time between the arrival of each peak of the waves, the greater the wavelength. And different wavelengths of light are perceived as having a different *hue* (what we usually mean by color, its qualitative aspect—red, green, etc.). We see very long wavelengths as red and very short ones as violet, with all other hues in between.

   Here's a particularly important fact: We don't see decreases in wavelength as a smooth shift in hue. Rather than being arranged along a single scale (for example, as is loudness, where increasingly greater amplitude produces increasingly louder sound), hue is psychologically arranged around a circle—the famous "color wheel." Some colors are nearby,

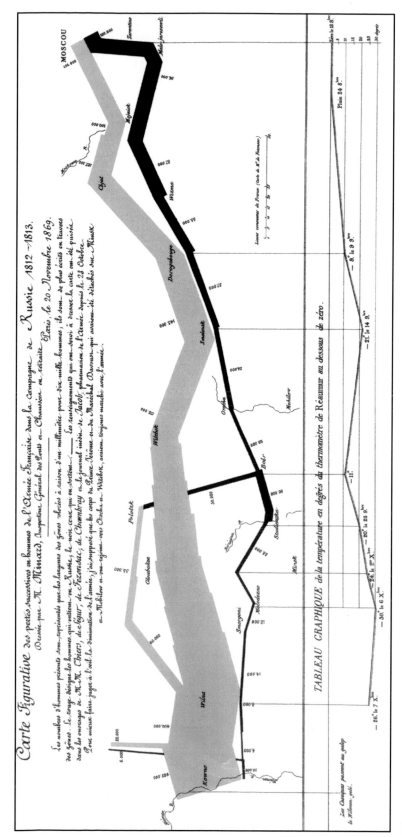

Figure 1.2, page 14. Minard's depiction of Napoleon's 1812 Russian campaign (From Tufte, 1983).

Figure 2.2, page 27. An opening slide that engages the audience and provides a general orientation. Although this is clearly a work of art, one can ask how it would function if it were intended to communicate—and point out some of the problems with using it in this way.

Figure 2.4, page 29. This slide acknowledges that many people have an overly narrow view of what psychology is and believe that it pertains only to psychotherapy. The audience needs to be disabused of this idea early in the presentation.

[**Don't**]

Don't vary color purely for decorative purposes

Figure 3.3a, page 65.

[**Do**]

Vary color only for emphasis or to group words together

Figure 3.3b, page 65.

Figure 3.7a, page 70.

Figure 3.7b, page 71. If the background is too salient, viewers will have to work to discriminate text from the background. A display should not be a haystack, with your message the needle. If you use a patterned background, make sure that it does not bury the text and that it is not so salient as to distract from your message.

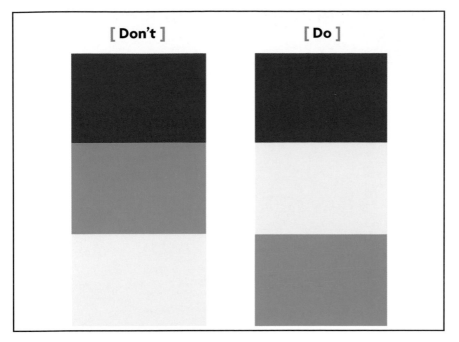

Figure 4.1, page 103. The eye cannot properly focus on red and blue at the same time, so the boundary between these colors shimmers.

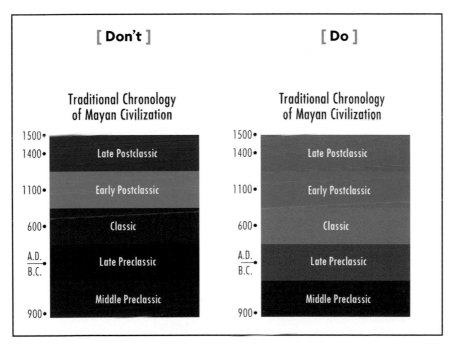

Figure 4.2. Equal lightnesses make boundaries harder to discern. A given level of intensity appears as different lightnesses to different people, and so differences in intensities must be large enough that all viewers will perceive distinct differences in lightness. (Note: The differences in lightness will probably be more evident in your PowerPoint slides than in this low-tech illustration.)

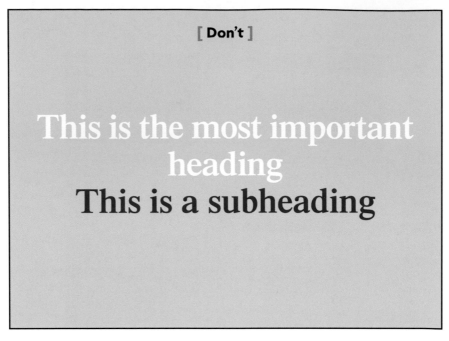

Figure 4.3a, page 105.

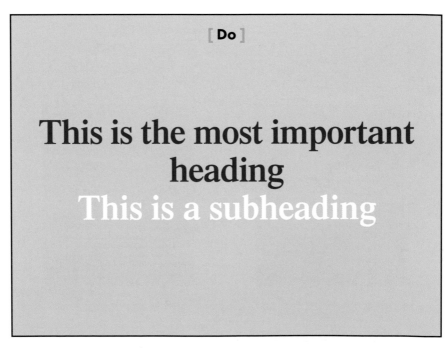

Figure 4.3b, page 105. The salience of colors should reflect the importance of the headings.

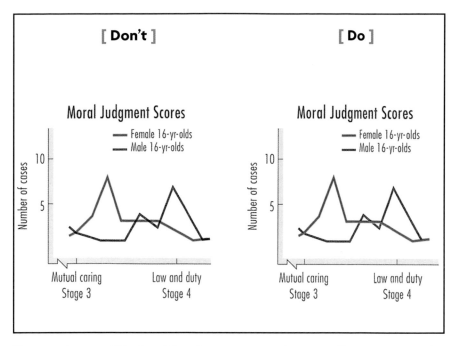

Figure 4.4, page 107. A red line that appears to be struggling to move to the foreground produces an effect that is neither aesthetically nor functionally desirable.

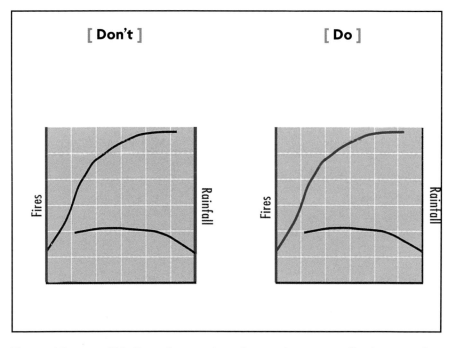

Figure 4.5, page 108. If used properly, color can be a very effective grouping device. In this example, color in the right panel groups the appropriate scale with the corresponding line.

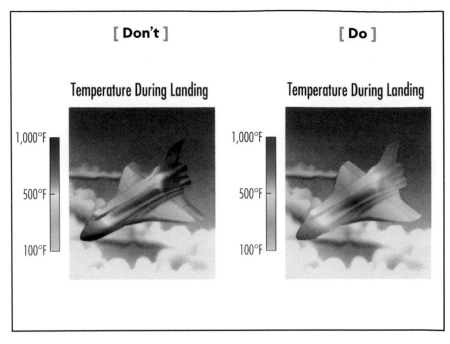

Figure 4.6, page 109. Because differences in hue are not immediately perceived as differences in amount, the viewer is required to memorize a key if hue alone is used to represent quantities (as in the version on the left). However, if the saturation and lightness vary along with hue, as in the version on the right, the viewer can easily see differences in represented amounts.

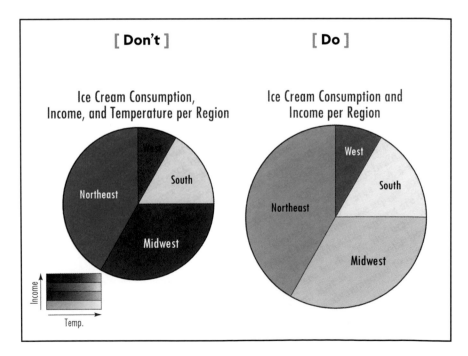

Figure 4.7, page 110. The display on the left uses size to indicate consumption by region, hue to indicate income, and saturation to indicate temperature; it is a puzzle to be solved. The display on the right uses only size and saturation to convey amounts, and viewers can clearly sense the orderings here.

others are opposite each other. Thus, it's not simple or straight-forward to use variations in hue to represent different quantities; changes in wavelength don't psychologically correspond to the impression of greater or smaller quantities.

2. The peaks of the light waves can be relatively high or low, which corresponds to the amount of light. That is called the lightness when the light is reflected (if the display is projected onto a screen) or brightness when the light is emitted (if the display is shown on a monitor). In either case, the amount of light can be varied by the amount of gray that is added. Here-after, I will use the term "lightness" to refer to the amount of light in the display, on the assumption that most presenta-tions will be projected, but the recommendations apply equally well to cases when presentations are shown on a monitor.

3. The purity of the color is its *saturation,* seen as the deepness of the color, which can be varied by the amount of white that is added. Adding white has the effect of "washing out" the hue, making it increasingly more subtle (such as in pastel colors). Saturation can be varied separately from lightness (as you can see on a monitor, when you turn up the intensity). And, unlike hue, both the lightness and saturation of a color can be varied quantitatively, producing the psychological impression that "more is more."

Color perception is complex in part because the perception of hue depends to some extent on the surrounding colors, and so the display must be looked at as a whole. Furthermore, people vary greatly in their perception of color. A sizable per-centage of the population (about 8 percent of American males and .5 percent of American females) is color-blind—that is, they have trouble distinguishing certain colors, typically red versus green. In addition, people vary greatly in their assessments of how intense two colors must be to have equal lightness.

The following recommendations will help you to ensure that the colors you use will be discriminable by everyone, that they don't irritate the viewer, and that they convey information properly.

1. Use colors that are well separated in the spectrum.

To increase discriminability, colors that are included in your display should be separated by at least one other noticeably distinct color in the spectrum, depicted in the color wheel. The six colors that we per-ceive as being most separated are *reddish-purple, blue, yellowish-gray, yellowish-green, red,* and *bluish-gray.* The "11 colors that are never confused" are *white, gray, black, red, green, yellow, blue, pink, brown, orange,* and *purple.*

But my strong advice is never to use all 11 in a single display: To do so would make the word "garish" seem inappropriately limp. Aesthetics aside, even when short-term memory limitations are not an issue (because the colors all are physically present), because in general people can easily keep in mind the differences among only nine colors.

2. Avoid using red and blue or red and green in adjacent regions.

In spite of the requirement that colors be well separated, and hence easily discriminable, you should not use hues that arise from very different wavelengths to define boundaries. The lens of the eye, unlike lenses in good cameras, cannot properly bring into focus two very different wavelengths at the same time. This is why red (a long wavelength) and blue (a relatively short wavelength) will seem to shimmer if juxtaposed. For most purposes, this effect will distract the viewer and should be avoided.

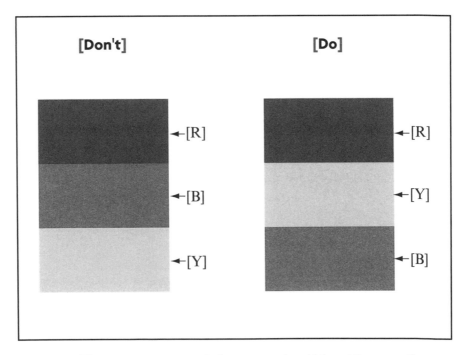

Figure 4.1. The eye cannot properly focus on red and blue at the same time, so a boundary should not be defined by juxtaposing red and blue regions. "R" is for red, "B" for blue, and "Y" for yellow. (See this figure in the color insert.)

In addition, it is usually a good idea to avoid using red and green to define a boundary, because a sizable percentage of the population has trouble distinguishing these colors (as noted earlier, this is the most common form of color-blindness).

3.   Make adjacent colors have different lightnesses.

Our visual systems have difficulty registering a boundary that is defined by two colors that have the same lightness. I discovered this the hard way while driving one winter dusk. A stop sign had been posted on a green steel girder that was holding up an overpass. The light was just right (i.e., wrong), and I didn't distinguish the red from the green—and was promptly pulled over and ticketed by a waiting patrolman. I decided that it really wasn't my fault; it was my all-too-human visual system's fault. So I went in to a preliminary hearing, to explain this to the magistrate. But seeing the look on his face after my mini-lecture, I gave up and paid the fine—and decided to be extra vigilant during dusk.

Unfortunately, you can't predict exactly how great the differences in lightness must be to discriminate boundaries between different hues easily. But, all else being equal, this may help: When colors reflect the same objective amount of light, we see blue as the lightest (or brightest) color, followed by red, green, yellow, and white. To be on the safe side, I recommend adjusting lightness subjectively, ensuring that it is obviously different in adjacent colors, for two reasons:

1. People vary considerably in their perception of how light a color is, and this can vary for different colors.
2. Different sorts of room lighting affect different colors in different ways.

4.   Ensure that the foreground and background are discriminable.

The 19th-century British genius Charles Babbage is credited with inventing the first calculating machine. Less well known is the fact that Babbage took extraordinary care before he published his table of logarithms in 1826, to the extent of testing the ease of reading 10 different colors of ink on 50 different colors of paper. The winner? The blackest ink on a light buff paper. In fact, the most discriminable colors are black and white. If you want to use these colors (perhaps because you are speaking in a huge room and want to ensure that even those at the very back can read your slides), consider how the room will be lit.

- If the room will be well lit, you are better off using black figures on a white background.
- If the room will be almost dark, a white background will appear very bright, perhaps even irritating (even if a light is shining on you, which I recommend). So, in this situation you generally are better off using white figures on a black background.

However, black and white are not the most exciting colors, and you won't lose much by using different hues for figure and background as long as they are clearly discriminable. To ensure that they are easily discriminable, be sure that the colors differ obviously in terms of all three qualities: hue, lightness, and saturation.

5. Make the most important content element the most salient.

Larger color differences will be noticed first, so ensure that the most important object or segment stands out the most.

- If no particular element is most important, make all elements equally salient.
- To make elements equally salient, after you adjust the hues and lightnesses so that the colors will be easily distinguished, adjust the saturations for the different hues you are using until none dominates.

6. Use one color for titles and another, less salient one for text.

To help the viewer organize your text, use one color (e.g., yellow-orange on a dark gray background) for titles and another color (e.g., white) for text entries beneath the title. But, as noted in Chapter 3, ensure that the title is a more salient color than the text, thereby appropriately directing the viewers' attention.

7. Use warm colors to define a foreground.

This recommendation is based on nonintuitive discoveries about visual perception. The brain senses depth in part by exploiting the slightly different images that are registered by each eye (because they are located in different places on the head). By analogy to a similar process in hearing, this is called *stereo vision*. Stereo vision works

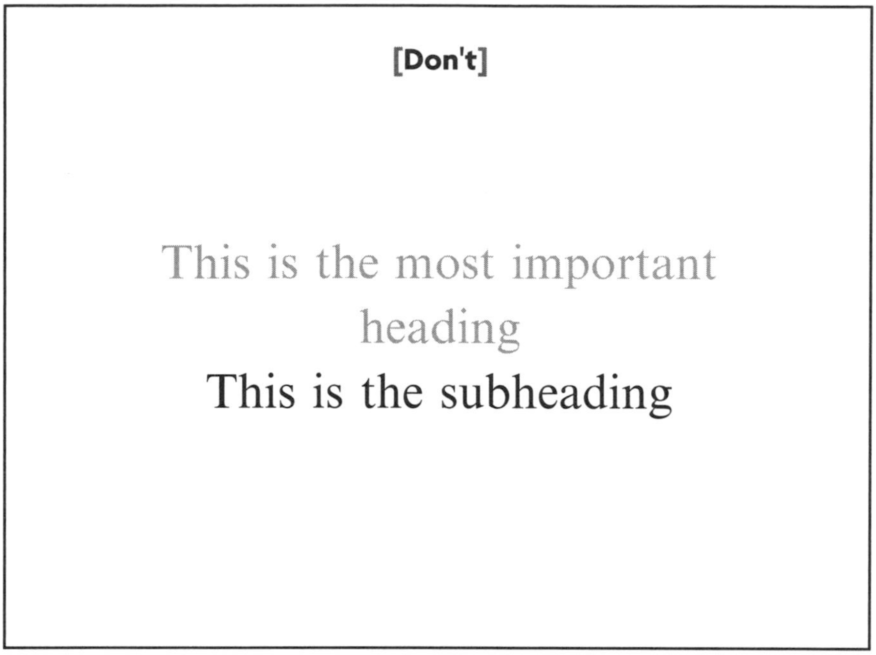

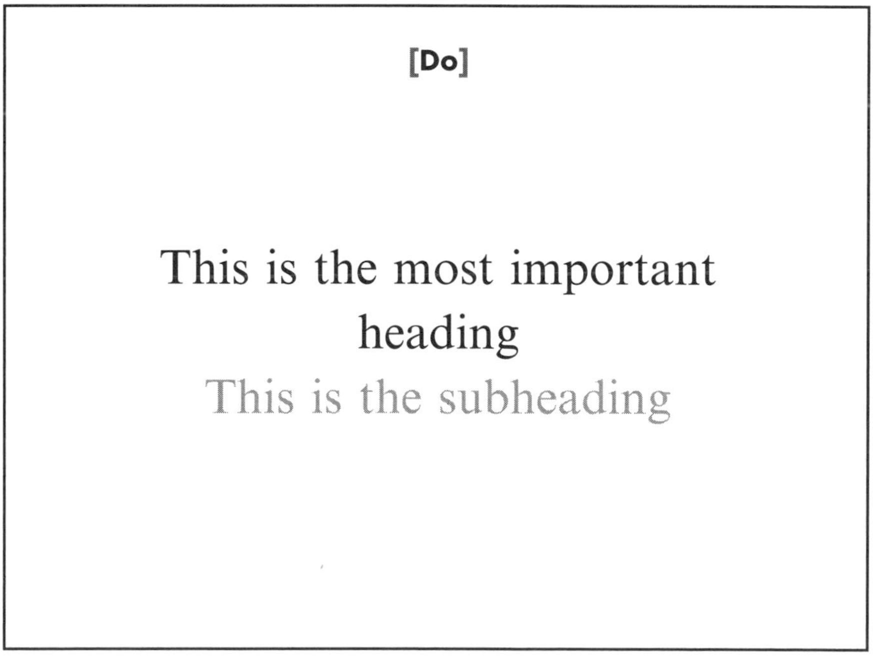

[Don't]

This is the most important heading

This is the subheading

[Do]

This is the most important heading

This is the subheading

Figure 4.3. The salience of colors should reflect the importance of the headings. (See the insert for the color versions of these figures.)

well to specify distance (up to about 10 feet away from the viewer), but it can be tricked to produce an interesting illusion. The illusion occurs because light waves usually contain a mixture of different wavelengths, which we see as different hues. You can separate out the different hues in ordinary light by holding a prism in front of a window and observing the rainbow that is projected on the wall. The lens of the eye acts like a prism because the eye is aimed slightly toward the center when we look at objects in front of us, and so the lens is angled. Light of different wavelengths is projected to slightly different locations on the back of the eye just as it is projected to slightly different locations on the wall when we hold up a prism. And this effect differs slightly for the two eyes, which produces a "false stereo" effect. The result: A "warm" color, such as red, yellow or orange, will appear to be in front of a "cooler" one, such as green, blue, or violet.

This odd fact about visual perception leads me to recommend that text should be a warmer color than the background, so that the background doesn't seem to fight to move in front of the text. Moreover, when two lines cross (as in Figure 4.4), the warmer one should pass over the cooler one; if it does not, the back line will seem to be struggling to come forward, trying to snake around the one in front. As entertaining as such effects may be, a good presentation is no place for a visual wrestling match!

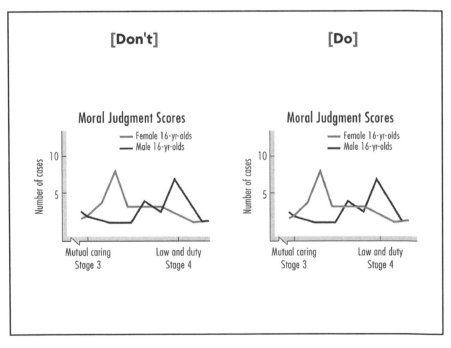

Figure 4.4. A red line that appears to be struggling to move to the foreground produces an effect that is neither esthetically nor functionally desirable (see this figure in the color insert).

8.   Don't use deep, heavily saturated blue for text or graphics.

Avoid rendering text or graphics in a deep, heavily saturated blue; the eye cannot focus the image properly, and so deep blues will appear blurred around the edges.

• Similarly, avoid cobalt blue, which is in fact a mixture of blue and red; for people with normal vision, this color can never be fully in focus because the eye cannot accommodate to both wavelengths at the same time. The halo you have probably noticed around blue street lights at night is not fog; your eyes are failing to focus the image properly.

9.   Use color to group elements.

Regions of the same color will be seen as a group. Use the same color for all titles and another color for all text entries, which will clearly group the material into these two categories. And use color to pair corresponding elements, as in Figure 4.5.

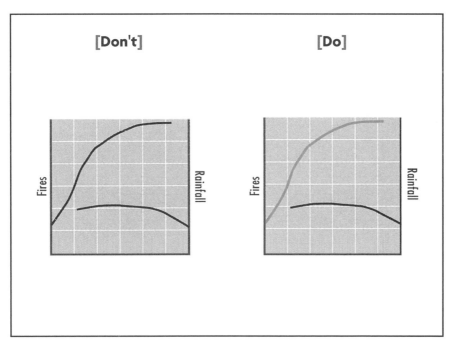

Figure 4.5. If used properly, color can be a very effective grouping device. In this example, color in the right panel groups the appropriate scale with the corresponding line (see this figure in the color insert).

Example: Grouping by similarity is very useful if you want the viewers to compare two or more elements in different places. For instance, if two pie graphs are used, using the same color for corresponding wedges will group them effectively.

10.   Increase saturation and lightness for hues that indicate greater amounts.

Don't vary hue by itself to represent differences in amounts. Using hue to represent amounts requires the viewer to memorize a key because hue itself does not vary along a continuum of less-to-more. For example, shifting from red to violet does not convey the impression that an amount has been added the way that shifting from a short bar to a tall bar does. Although the wavelengths of the hues order them into red, orange, yellow, green, blue, indigo, and violet, hues are not a psychological continuum.

In some situations you may need to use hue to convey quantitative information, such as occurs in pictures of the brain that indicate the amount of activation when a person performs some task, or pictures of a model airplane in a wind tunnel that indicate the relative friction along different surfaces. In such cases, color is used to specify quantities associated with each portion of an object.

- For such graphics, use deeper saturations (more color) and greater lightnesses (more light) for hues that indicate greater amounts. We see increases in both of these visual dimensions as increases in amount, and so these increases can signal increasing quantities effectively.
- If you must use hue to convey variations in quantity (e.g., to show variations in temperature across a complex surface), use psychologically equal changes in color to convey equal increments in the amount—and you'll need to experiment to get this approximately right. If the psychological increments don't seem about equal, viewers will assume that more similar quantities are conveyed by more similar colors.

11.   Don't use hue, lightness, and saturation to specify different measurements.

The recommendation to co-vary the three aspects of color to indicate greater amounts will also lead you to avoid using hue (the qualitative aspect of color), lightness (the amount of light), and saturation (the deepness) to convey different types of information.

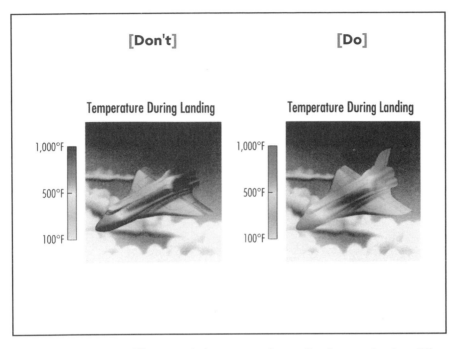

Figure 4.6. Because differences in hue are not immediately perceived as differences in amount, the viewer is required to memorize a key if hue alone is used to represent quantities (as in the version on the left). However, if the saturation and lightness vary along with hue, as in the version on the right, the viewer can easily see differences in represented amounts (see this figure in the color insert).

- Don't be tempted to specify three different types of measurements in a single graphic. The viewer will have a very difficult time sorting them out because hue and lightness, and hue and saturation, are so-called integral perceptual dimensions (they group together perceptually; see the discussion of the Principle of Perceptual Organization in the appendix). A viewer looking at a colored region cannot help but pay attention to its depth and lightness as well as its hue.

12. Respect compatibility and conventions of color.

A friend of mine was teaching a seminar on the cultural revolution in China. I asked him what color he was using for the background in his PowerPoint slides, and he said, "Red." When I asked him to describe the color in more detail, he said that it in fact was more like a burgundy. This was a wise choice, for two reasons:

1. Fire-engine red is a warm color and will be seen as closer than cooler colors—not a good idea for a background.

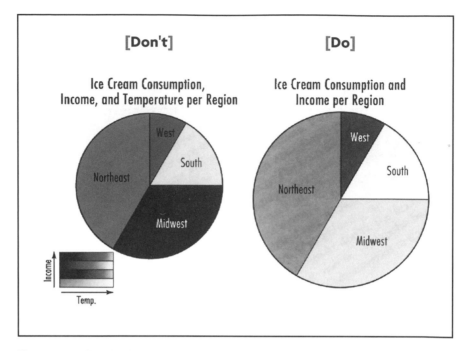

Figure 4.7. The display on the left uses size to indicate consumption by region, hue to indicate income, and saturation to indicate temperature; it is a puzzle to be solved. The display on the right uses only size and saturation to convey amounts, and viewers can clearly sense the orderings here (see this figure in the color insert).

2. However, using a shade of red is compatible with the topic, red being the color of the Chinese revolution.

Objects and events sometimes have characteristic colors, different cultures have specific conventional color symbols, and colors may also have political connotations, for example, in the United States, "red states" are conservative, and "blue states" are liberal. Although the colors probably were not intended to convey specific connotations, we nevertheless can ask what red and blue signify in the United States. The best survey I know of on this topic was conducted by Joe Hallock (http://joehallock.com/edu/COM498/credits. html). Here are some of his survey results, indicating the percentage of people who associated the colors with the concepts (for example, he asked them to indicate which color "best represents trust"). I've focused here just on blue and red:

Concept	Blue	Red
Trust:	34	6
Security:	28	9
Speed:	1	76
High quality:	20	3
Reliability/dependability:	43	3
Fear/terror:	0	41
Fun:	5	16
Favorite color:	42	8
Least favorite:	0	1

In short, for Americans, blue is generally a more desirable color. But even this depends on the specific message you want to present; if you want to convey speed, fear, or fun, red would be more effective.

Texture: 2 Points Regarding Hatching

Individual bars in bar graphs, wedges of pie graphs, regions of maps, or portions of diagrams are often filled with a textured pattern. The following two recommendations will help you make helpful hatchings.

1. Ensure that textures are discriminable.

As discussed, if neighboring regions are too close in color, the brain will not easily establish a border between them. (That's why a polar bear lying on the snow is hard to see. Camouflage is advantageous to a polar bear, not to a display.) By the same token, if two regions differ only by their texture, the brain will not easily establish a border between them if the textures are too similar. Here's how to ensure that textured regions are easily discriminable:

- *Vary orientation by at least 30 degrees of tilt.* When you read an analog clock (one with hands, not just numbers), some positions of the hands require closer attention than others. In accordance with the Principle of Perceptual Organization (specifically, the aspect of Input Channels; see the appendix for details), if differently oriented hatchings are used to distinguish regions, their tilts should differ by at least 30 degrees (the angle formed by the hands of a clock when they point to adjacent numbers, as at 12:05; see Figure 4.8).
- *Vary the spacing of texture patterns with similar orientations by at least a ratio of 2 to 1.* If cross-hatching, stripes, dots, dashes, or other regular patterns have similar orientations (that is, within 30

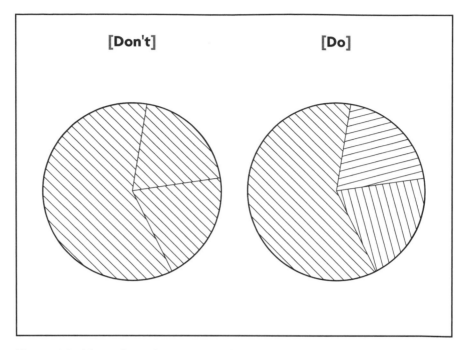

Figure 4.8. Line orientations must be immediately discriminable to delineate regions clearly.

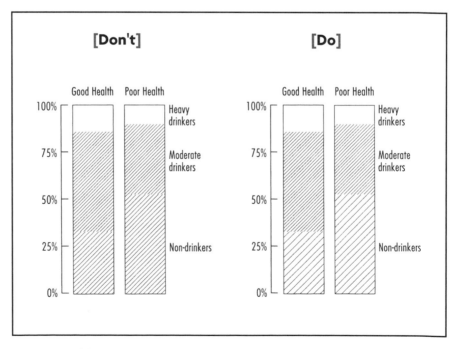

Figure 4.9. Line spacings that differ by at least a 2:1 ratio are immediately discriminable; if regions are not immediately discriminable, the viewer has to work harder than necessary to compare corresponding elements.

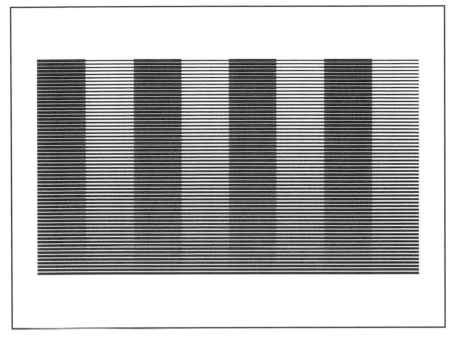

Figure 4.10. An annoying shimmer occurs when your visual system is struggling to detect a poorly defined edge.

degrees of each other), the densities of the pattern should differ by at least 2-to-1 (Figure 4.9). If a region has 8 hatch lines to the inch, to be immediately discriminable adjacent regions should have either 4 or fewer lines to the inch, or 16 or more lines to the inch.

2.   Avoid visual beats.

Similarly oriented patterns of stripes or texture elements may appear to shimmer, a distracting and irritating effect (Figure 4.10).This effect is less likely to happen if the stripes of texture elements in different regions are easily discriminable, as specified in the previous recommendation.

Filling: 3 Points about Background Patterns

In many PowerPoint displays, the background contains a pattern, which is included primarily to make the display more attractive or interesting. If you choose to use a pattern for your background, such as those provided in the PowerPoint templates, be careful to ensure that it does not obscure the message.

1. Ensure that the background pattern is not salient.

Every once in a while I see a movie with an actor so talented that a minor character "steals the show" (think of Bill Nighy's role as Billy Mack in *Love Actually*). Don't let this happen to your presentation, where the background is so interesting that it steals the show. The background should not distract from the information-bearing lines and regions, nor should its salience lure the eye away from these elements. A background should be lighter and in less saturated colors than those used in the rest of the display, have few details, and have soft edges.

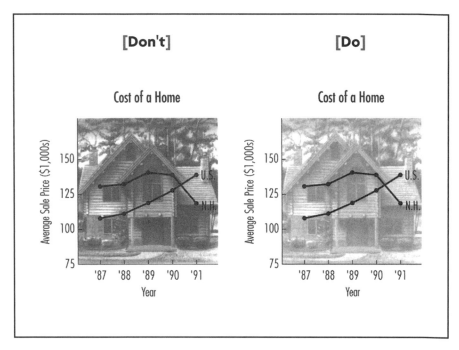

Figure 4.11. If salience leads readers to see the house before the data, they will have to work to sort out the content.

2. Don't allow parts of background patterns to group with parts of the foreground.

Use contrasting hue, saturation, and brightness to ensure that background figures don't group with parts of the display itself, producing confusion between background figures and content (Figure 4.12).

3. Use a background pattern to reinforce the main point of the presentation.

An effective background can underline (as opposed to undermine) the overarching message of the presentation, providing a kind of pictorial

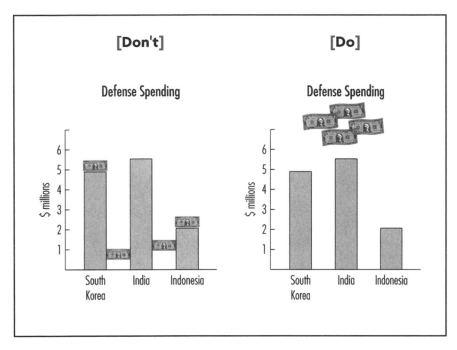

Figure 4.12. If background elements group with content, the display is likely to be misinterpreted.

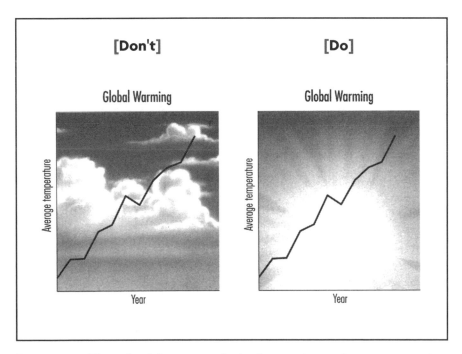

Figure 4.13. The editorial content of a background can allow you to underline your message effectively, or it can create confusion; the background pattern should not conflict with the message of the display.

label (Figure 4.13). In order to be effective, the background design must be compatible with the content of the presentation. To get a quick sense of whether you are on track, show a couple of friends the background image that you are considering using and ask them to describe it; this description should be appropriate for the topic and should have connotations that are compatible with your message.

- Every element of a display should convey information (such as the fact that amounts are specified in U.S. dollars in Figure 4.12). Tacked-on elements—such as pictures of the planets or swirls of different colors—will only distract the viewers.

Animation and Transitions: 10 Recommendations

Recently, I experienced one of the most disheartening things that can happen during a presentation: One of the audience members seated near the front of the room stood up and left during the middle of my presentation. Her standing up and then walking the length of the aisle to the exit was not only an apparent comment on my presentation (she was "voting with her feet"), but it also caught the attention of the rest of the audience. I had to speak a bit more loudly, and be a bit more animated for a moment, or I would have lost even more of the audience as their attention was distracted. But it wasn't their fault; the human brain is wired so that change—including change in position—automatically catches our attention. This makes animation (i.e., movement of a pattern on a screen) a two-edged sword: It can be used to direct the viewers' attention to what you want to say, or it can distract them from your message. My recommendations focus on ways to ensure that animation does in fact work for you, not against you.

1.   Use animation to direct attention.

If you are discussing a sequence of events that you've represented graphically, use animation to guide the viewers sequentially through the graphic.

Example: If you present a flowchart, have the arrows appear only when the transition from one phase to another becomes relevant, and have the arrows literally grow from the process (box in the chart) just being discussed to the next one.

- Even if you are not discussing a sequence of events, you can use motion to guide attention: In general, presenting a label first and then having an arrow extend from the label until it touches the labeled part is an effective way to direct the viewers' attention.

2. Use novel transitions to catch attention.

The PowerPoint program provides many options for transitions between slides, such as by having a slide enter from the left or by having it built up from fragments that come together. The first time you use a transition, the novelty will grab the viewers' attention. Change of any sort should carry information—and such change does: The information being "Wake up and pay attention! This is especially important!" But after that, the audience will adapt and come to expect that transition—and a new type of transition would be necessary to grab their attention later, to emphasize yet something else that's important. I would not recommend making such changes more than once or twice during your presentation, however; people adapt quickly, and what changes can soon become what's staying the same. As the French put it, *plus ça change, plus c'est la même chose*—the more things change, the more they stay the same.

3. Don't randomly use different transitions for different slides.

Use the same transitions throughout the presentation, unless you want to emphasize a particular slide (as noted above). Don't change the type of transition randomly.

4. In general, don't use slow fade-in or fade-out.

The PowerPoint program allows you to make a slide fade in or fade out. If this is rapid (less than 1 second), it is simply another form of transition. But if a slide slowly becomes visible (taking more than 1 second to appear fully), the viewers first will see parts that are not immediately discriminable, which will require either that they work to read the slide or that they wait until it is clear. Neither situation is ideal, and you risk allowing the viewers' attention to wander.

Some presenters use a slow fade to give viewers a moment or two to absorb complex information. However, in this situation I recommend simply leaving the slide visible until you think they have understood the material.

5.   Don't move portions of the same text line or graphic separately.

Move portions of the same piece of information (text or graphic) in the same way, so that they group together.

Example: If each bulleted item in a list enters from the left, ensure that all words in an entry come in together. Having them arrive one at a time, or from different locations, only makes the viewer have to work in order to organize them into an interpretable unit.

6.   Don't move more than four separate perceptual groups simultaneously.

To avoid overloading our ability to track and hold in mind information, don't have more than four groups (defined by the Principle of Perceptual Organization) moving at the same time.

7.   Don't require viewers to read moving words.

Ask anyone who has ever stood in Times Square in New York City and tried to read the news on the ticker-tape display: Moving words are hard to track and interpret. Any gain in visual interest is more than canceled by the added processing difficulty.

8.   Build up complex displays a part at a time.

If you are showing a complex display, you can help the viewers by using animation to build it up, a part at a time (while keeping the portions of each part together, as already noted). Having a part enter from the top ensures that the viewers will focus on just that new part, and then see how it is integrated into the whole.

Example: If you were showing a map of the southern states and wanted to indicate average weekly coffee consumption per capita, you might use icons of stacks of coffee cups to indicate the amount (each cup would signify a certain amount of consumption, ideally one cup). Each stack would be built up as coffee cups dropped down from the top, one at a time onto a specific state, with the final height indicating the average amount of coffee consumed. If the precise amount were important, you could have the numerical value appear at the top of the stack after the cups had slid down to their proper resting places. Using animation in this way will direct the viewers' attention to just the material you want to discuss at any one point.

9. Make animations compatible with the represented object or event.

Many objects and events have characteristic movements, which should be preserved in the way you have them move on the screen.

Example: If you show a picture of an automobile, don't have it rise up from the bottom of the screen or seem to drop down from the sky. Have it enter from the left if it faces to the right, or from the right if it faces to the left. Similarly, if you want to use the height of a flower to indicate the amount of rainfall, have the flower grow vertically.

10. Use videoclips to illustrate a relevant event.

When integrated into a PowerPoint presentation, video clips can illustrate an event that unfolds over time better than a description or set of still slides. All of the recommendations regarding Clipart in the following chapter also apply to video clips. In addition, a word to the wise: Be sure that your video will in fact operate on the computer you are using—videoclips are memory-intensive and will not run on all machines.

Sound: 10 Ways to Avoid Making Noise

The PowerPoint program allows you to present sounds, either from a built-in menu of choices (which includes sounds such as a dog barking or a man laughing) or custom-defined. The following 10 recommendations apply to the use of sounds.

1. Use sounds to grab the audience's attention.

An unexpected or distinctive sound typically has the same effect as a sudden motion: It grabs the audience members' attention. However, unlike motion, sounds don't inherently direct the audience to a specific item on a slide. Rather, sounds alert the audience to another event, such as a change in text or graphics. If a slide has been visible for a few minutes, and only a portion of the slide is then changed, an appropriate sound will help to draw the viewers' attention to the change.

> **Example:** If you want to show how lightning can spark a forest fire, you may first need to show the audience a picture of a forest and describe the relevant conditions. If this takes you a few minutes, you might then want to present an audible "crack" when you show the lightning bolt.

2.   Use sounds sparingly as alerts.

If you use sound to grab attention, do so sparingly. The first time you do this, it will wake up the audience and alert them to the upcoming event. By the third time you do this, the audience may become annoyed—and may even begin to filter out the sound.

3.   Use sounds to define the context.

Sounds can set the stage for your entire presentation, a portion of your presentation, or a specific point. These sounds should be very transitory, however, functioning as a kind of auditory title.

> **Example**: If you are talking about pollution in the seas, you can start with the sound of surf. Or if you are talking about the growing barter economy, you can play the sound of an open-air market. Both National Public Radio (NPR) and the British Broadcasting Corporation (BBC) radio news make very effective use of such sounds to set the stage for their feature stories.

4.   Use sounds that are appropriate for the topic and point being made.

If you use a sound to introduce a slide, ensure that it is compatible with the point.

> **Example**: If you want to introduce a presentation or section on the effects of a hurricane, the sounds of a ferocious wind might be appropriate, especially if accompanied by a video clip of the wind ripping through a town. The sounds of gentle rain on the roof would not be appropriate.

- If you use an inappropriate sound, it will seem funny—which is not always a bad thing, but you should intend this effect, not fall victim to it.
- My advice: Never, ever use rude or crude sounds (you know what they are).

5.   Use sounds to allow the audience to "come up for air".

Sounds can serve as a kind of punctuation in a complex presentation (again, NPR and BBC radio are very good at doing this); giving the audience a chance to "come up for air" allows them to process the information you've just presented.

> **Example:** If you've been presenting data on emerging stock markets in the former Soviet Union, you might have a few seconds of the sound of the floor of one of the exchanges, accompanying an appropriate title on a slide, such as "Russian Stock Exchanges."

- However, you should use sound in this way only very sparingly, and your timing must bc just right. Otherwise you will not seem serious, and the audience will discount your message.

6.   Use sounds to provide evidence.

In spite of the ample evidence to the contrary (served up daily by creative artists armed with computer graphics programs), for most people seeing is believing. The same goes for many sorts of sounds. Sounds, especially recorded dialogues, can serve the same roles as photographs when used as evidence.

> **Example**: If you want to illustrate typical interactions between physicians and patients, brief sound clips that provide samples of such interactions might be appropriate.

7.   Coordinate sounds, text, and graphics.

Although you can show a blank background slide when you present sounds, doing so misses a valuable opportunity to provide the audience with dual means of learning the material, via sight and sound. It's best to present sounds with appropriate visuals. If you are presenting sounds as evidence, the ultimate example of coordinating sounds with graphics is a video clip, where the audience sees the sources of the sounds.

- If the sounds are discrete, such as the sounds different animals make, show a photo of each object, and click on the graphic to present the corresponding sound (assuming that this is relevant to your message).

8.   Don't arbitrarily vary tonal quality or volume.

If you use sounds, ensure that they all have the same tonal quality and are presented at the same volume—unless changing the quality or volume is part of your message. Any perceptible change will be taken to signal information, and thus arbitrary changes will be confusing and distracting.

9.   Ensure that sounds can be heard clearly throughout the room.

As usual, the material must be discriminable, and the sounds must be loud enough to be heard by all.

- In addition, don't make the sounds too loud, which will not only cause the audience members to cringe, but may lead them to anticipate further assaults and thus not pay close attention to your message.

10.   Ensure that sounds are high fidelity.

A common problem with presenting sounds is that most computers have poor speakers, so that the sounds can be muddy and difficult to understand. Avoid this problem by ensuring that you have good external speakers, which should have independent amplifiers.

From the Principles to the Point

The key to these recommendations is the psychological principles. In what follows I revisit the principles and note which ones contributed primarily to each of the major recommendations I offer.

Principle of Relevance: Communication is most effective when neither too much nor too little information is presented. (We understand and remember a message more easily when the right amount of detail is used to make the point.)

- Use sounds to provide evidence.

Principle of Appropriate Knowledge: Communication requires prior knowledge of pertinent concepts, jargon, and symbols. (We understand and remember a message more easily if it connects to what we already know.)

- Use video clips to illustrate a relevant event.
- Use sounds that are appropriate for the topic and point being made.
- Use sounds to define the context.

Principle of Salience: Attention is drawn to large perceptible differences. (Big relative differences grab attention.)

- Make the most important content element the most salient.
- Use one color for titles and another, less salient one for text.
- Use warm colors to define a foreground.
- Ensure that the background pattern is not salient.
- Use animation to direct attention.
- Use novel transitions to catch attention.
- Use sounds to grab the audience's attention.
- In general, don't use transitions in which slides slowly appear or fade out.

Principle of Discriminability: Two properties must differ by a large enough proportion or they will not be distinguished. (We need contrast to distinguish shapes, colors, or positions from each other and from the background.)

- Use colors that are well separated in the spectrum.
- Avoid using red and blue in adjacent regions.
- Make adjacent colors have different lightnesses.
- Ensure that the foreground and background are discriminable.
- Don't use deep, heavily saturated blue for text or graphics.
- Ensure that textures are discriminable.
- Avoid visual beats.
- Ensure that sounds can be heard clearly throughout the room.
- Ensure that sounds are high fidelity.

Principle of Perceptual Organization: People automatically group elements into units, which they then attend to and remember. (These groups are easier to see and remember than the isolated components would be.)

- Use color to group elements.

- Don't use hue, lightness, and saturation to specify different measurements.
- Don't allow parts of background patterns to group with parts of the foreground.
- Vary the orientation of similar texture elements in different regions by at least 30 degrees of tilt.
- Vary the spacing of texture elements with similar orientations in different regions by a ratio of at least two to one.
- Don't move portions of the same text line or graphic separately.

Principle of Compatibility: A message is easiest to understand if its form is compatible with its meaning. (For better or worse, the mind tends to judge a book by its cover.)

- Avoid using hue to represent quantitative information.
- Increase saturation and lightness for hues that indicate greater amounts.
- Respect compatibility and conventions of color.
- Make animations compatible with the represented object or event.
- Use sounds that are appropriate for the topic and point being made.
- Use a background pattern to reinforce the main point of the presentation.
- Coordinate sounds, text, and graphics.

Principle of Informative Changes: People expect changes in properties to carry information. (And we expect every necessary piece of information to be indicated by a change in a perceptible property.)

- Don't randomly use different transitions for different slides.
- Use sounds sparingly as alerts.
- Don't arbitrarily vary tonal quality or volume.

Principle of Capacity Limitations: People have a limited capacity to retain and to process information and so will not understand a message if too much information must be retained or processed. (From a communicative point of view, less can be more!)

- Build up complex displays a part at a time.
- Don't move more than four separate perceptual groups simultaneously.
- Use sounds to allow the audience to "come up for air."
- Don't require viewers to read moving words.

Communicating Quantitative Information: Graphs

5

In 1978 I was contacted by a small company called Consulting Statisticians, Inc. They had received a request for proposals issued by the National Institute of Education. Someone in the government had apparently noticed that many people could not read charts and graphs very well and wanted to spark more research on the topic. I was intrigued. Then-graduate student Steven Pinker and I wrote a proposal, and it was funded. So began my work on graphs. That work ultimately led to the eight principles that guide the recommendations in this book, and graphs serve as a prototype for how to apply those principles.

Graphs are pictures intended to convey information about numbers and relationships among numbers. Graphs can convey the information in a large set of numbers more effectively than just listing the numbers—or can fail miserably. In this chapter I help you avoid making graphs that confuse rather than illuminate, and instead will guide you to make graphs that could be worth many numbers—becoming pictures that are truly worth 1,000 words.

To Graph or Not to Graph? The 3 Big Questions

The following considerations will help you to decide whether you should use a graph or would be better off with a table or text.

1. Do you want to illustrate relative amounts?

If so, then a graph is appropriate. Graphs can also specify specific amounts (in labels at specific points), but what they do best is to exploit the "more-is-more" rule: We automatically see larger wedges, longer bars, or higher points along a line as signifying greater quantities, and it's easy for us to see relative differences along these visual dimensions.

2. Do you have data needed for a specific purpose?

If your data address a specific issue, then a graph can be illuminating. Decide what questions audience members should be able to answer from the display, and organize the data accordingly. As usual, don't include any more or less information than is needed to answer the relevant questions.

Example: If you want the audience members to know whether sales are increasing at the same rates in different parts of the country, plotting the data separately for each of your product lines would only be an obstacle; audience members would mentally have to average over lots of lines or bars to obtain the information they needed. On the other hand, if you want the audience to know about differences in sales of commercial and personal equipment, it would be an error not to include separate bars or lines for each type. There is no way of mentally breaking down a single point or bar into its constituent parts.

3. Can you use concepts and display formats that are familiar to the audience?

If not, then a graph will not serve you well. I was shocked when I discovered that a substantial number of undergraduates at Harvard University don't really know how to read line graphs. The "more-is-more" rule has been a revelation for some of these students. Don't assume that even an intelligent and presumably well-educated audience will necessarily understand information graphics. If you decide to use a graph:

- Pick a display format that's familiar to a particular audience. When in doubt, explain how the graphic works.
- Use concepts familiar to that audience.
- In general, stick to the tried-and-true, "traditional" graphs that I discuss in this chapter.

In the remaining sections of this chapter, we will consider pie graphs, visual tables, line graphs, bar graphs, step graphs, scatterplots, and multi-panel displays.

Pie Graphs: 6 Tips

The pie graph is the most common format that shows how a whole is divided into parts. The relative area of each component, the wedge, represents the proportion of the whole taken by the component.

1. Use a pie to convey approximate relative amounts.

Yogi Berra once commented that "Baseball is 90 percent mental. The other half is physical." He would never have made this blooper if he had tried to use a pie graph to express this idea. And you'll never make similar gaffes if you display such data in a pie graph, which illustrates proportions of a whole. The main drawback to pie graphs is that it's often difficult to obtain relatively precise amounts from them, such as the percentage of one part. However, this is not a problem if the amount is 25 percent, 50 percent or 75 percent, which are easy to discern at a glance. If other amounts are illustrated, the precise amounts will not be easy to obtain because it is difficult visually for us to measure the angle, chord (i.e., straight line that connects the two sides of the wedge at the point where those lines meet the surrounding circle—making the wedge into a triangle), or area of each wedge precisely.

> **Example:** It is easy to use the "Do" graph in Figure 5.1 to get a general sense of the relative proportions, but difficult to use the "Don't" graph to determine that there were 13 percent more car and mobile home loans than bank and finance loans.

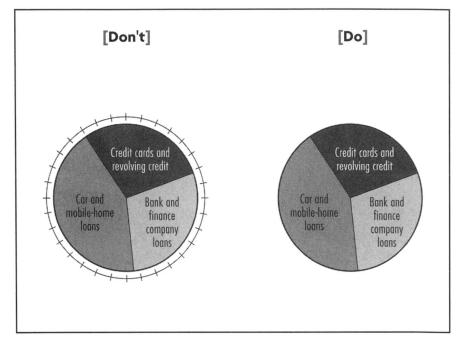

Figure 5.1. Do not use a scale with pie graphs; the viewer will have to struggle to count the number of ticks. In this graph, credit cards and revolving credit are the topic of interest, and hence this information is most salient.

2.   Label wedges if precise values are important.

A good way to convey precise amounts while still depicting relative proportions with pie graphs is simply to label the wedges, either by putting the numbers in them (if space permits) or next to them. This converts the pie into a hybrid display, part pie and part table.

3.   Use an exploded pie to emphasize a small proportion of parts.

Construct an exploded pie display by displacing the important slice or slices, as if a wedge of pizza had been pulled out from the pie. If the audience is supposed to make only approximate visual comparisons, the pie format provides a particularly good way to draw attention to a small percentage of the total number of components.

> **Example:** Look at the "Do" graph in Figure 5.2; it is immediately obvious that credit cards and revolving credit are the most important aspects of the display. In contrast, in the "Don't" version it is not clear what the audience should focus on.

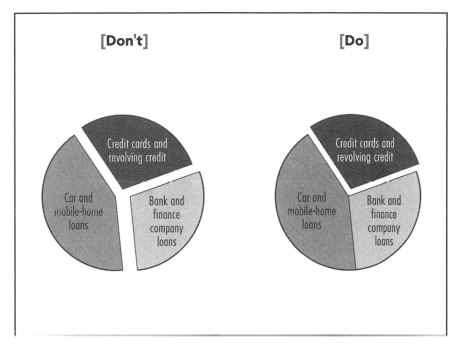

Figure 5.2. Use an exploded pie only when a distinct contour can be disrupted by exploding the wedges; the two intact pieces of the pie on the right define a contour, which makes the exploded wedge stand out.

4.   Explode a maximum of 25 percent of the wedges.

If you decide to use an exploded pie, you must decide which part or parts to emphasize. If too many wedges are exploded, as they are in "Don't," of Figure 5.3, the viewers won't know where to look. I once saw a cat freeze in confusion when it knocked over a trash can and some half-dozen mice scattered in different directions; it just didn't seem to know which one to pounce on. Don't make your viewers like that cat. I offer 25 percent as a rough guideline; there is no hard-and-fast percentage. The critical consideration is that enough wedges remain in the pie to make the exploded wedges appear to disrupt the contour of the whole.

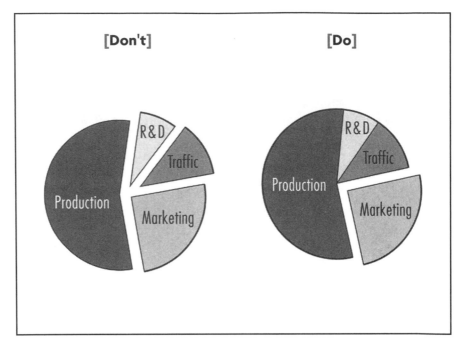

Figure 5.3. If too many wedges are exploded, none stands out.

5. Arrange wedges in a simple progression.

Unless there are reasons to order the wedges in a specific way, it will be easiest to compare the wedges if they are arranged in order of size (see Figure 5.4).

- In general, order from smaller to larger, with size increasing clockwise. Because values on a clock face increase in a clockwise direction, we expect greater quantities to be indicated by greater arcs in a clockwise direction.
- However, if you wish to emphasize the larger components, put the largest at the top or in the "1:00" position (the first that the viewer will focus upon when scanning in a clockwise order), and arrange the other wedges in decreasing size from this anchor point.

6. If proportions vary greatly, don't use multiple pies to compare corresponding parts.

Compare the two pies in the "Don't" version of Figure 5.5. How did Peugeot and Renault do in the European Community (EC) in general

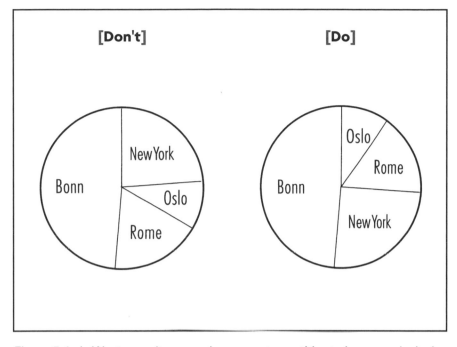

Figure 5.4. In Western culture, readers expect quantities to increase clockwise around a circle.

(left) compared with Italy in particular (right)? (These data were cited in 1991, prior to the formation of the European Union.) This is difficult to fathom, in part because the relevant wedges are in different locations in the two pies—a shift that cannot be avoided when the proportions vary widely.

Now compare the two "Do" pie graphs; it is clear that there is a rough correspondence between the revenues per region (left) and employees per region (right). It is easy to compare multiple pies when the wedges are in roughly the same positions in each. But, as illustrated in "Don't," when the corresponding parts are in different locations, the audience is forced to search for them one at a time—which requires effort. Our brains have limited processing capacity, and if forced to strain, many audience members may simply give up. (Also note that because Western Europe was of greatest interest to the designers, the largest wedge is put at the beginning of the clockwise progression.)

- If the proportions are very different across levels, and the audience is supposed to compare specific components, a bar graph is the preferable format.

[Don't]

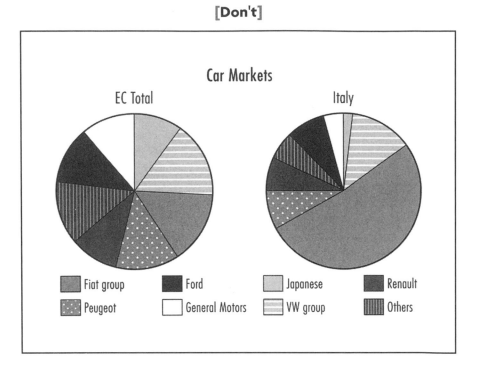

[Do]

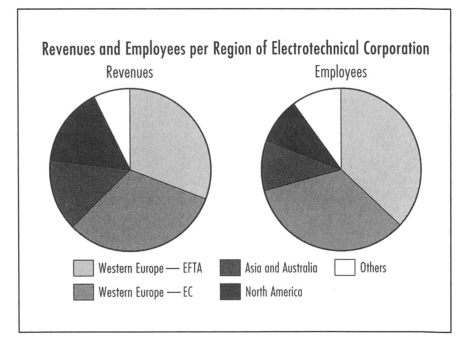

Figure 5.5. Corresponding wedges are hard to compare if, as in "Car Markets," they are not in corresponding positions.

Visual Tables: 8 More Legs to Stand On

We now turn to visual tables, which are pared-down graphs; objects are drawn so that their sizes or numbers vary in accordance with the amount being represented. Some visual tables use pictures of actual objects, and some use abstract content such as bars (without axes or scales).

1.   Use a visual table to convey impressions of relative amounts.

If you want the audience to gain only a general sense of the ordering of measurements, a visual table is appropriate.

Example: Stacks of small water bottles, varying in number, may be enough to illustrate the increase in consumption over time.

2.   Don't use the area of elements to convey precise quantities.

Because visual tables don't have scales, and because the visual system tends to distort our impression of the sizes of areas, don't use visual tables to depict precise amounts.

3.   Provide labels to specify relevant precise amounts.

If precise values are important, label each content element with its amount (in the same way that you can label the sizes of individual pie wedges).

Example: If the numbers of balloons (presumably filled with hot air) indicate the number of speeches delivered by each of several politicians, you could draw a bunch of balloons for each pol, with a tag on the bottom that indicates the name of the politician and the actual number of speeches.

But be careful: This practice can easily result in a cluttered display, relegating the content elements to the role of mere decorations. If you want to convey precise numbers, consider simply using a tabular format instead.

4. Use sets of icons to provide labels or to compare relative amounts.

A special case of a visual table is the *isotype*, in which bars are created by repeating small pictures, each of which corresponds to a specific amount of the measured substance. These displays have two particular uses:

1. Pictures can provide a direct label of what's been measured, which reduces processing required to search for verbal labels.
2. Different pictures can indicate component parts of the measured entity.

Example: You could specify the number of male and female employees in the different divisions of a company (see Figure 5.6) by showing a column that contains copies of a male icon versus a column that contains copies of a female icon (perhaps of the sort that often grace the corresponding restroom doors) above a label for each division; each picture would stand for an increment of, say, five employees, with more pictures (forming a

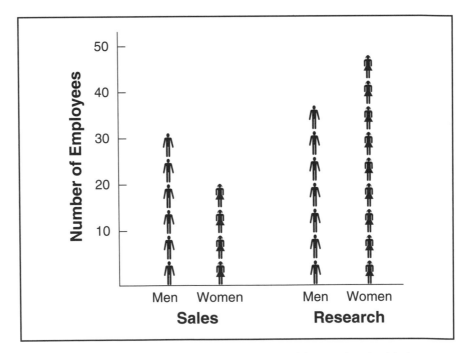

Figure 5.6. This bar graph could easily be turned into a visual table because the icons neatly label the bars, making the labels on the X-axis superfluous if the context in which the display is presented is clear enough. In this graph, each icon represents five employees, but the unit size is determined both by the ease of identifying the icons (if they are too small, they will not be discriminable) and the precision of the data.

higher stack) indicating more of that type of employee in that division. You can present precise amounts by showing a portion of an icon at the top of a stack, but be sensitive to how you truncate: A headless man at the top might lead audiences to draw the wrong conclusions about the quality of the staff! (In this case, make the top icon appropriately shorter by removing parts of the torso and legs—or just round off and only show intact icons, noting that you've done this in an explanatory note at the bottom or under the title.)

5. Make the appearance of the pattern compatible with what it symbolizes.

Don't fight human nature: Make the cover fit the book. If the properties of a pattern are not compatible with its meaning, the audience will have to work to understand the display. The visual impression of an amount or a difference should correspond to the actual amount or difference between the represented substances (Figure 5.7).

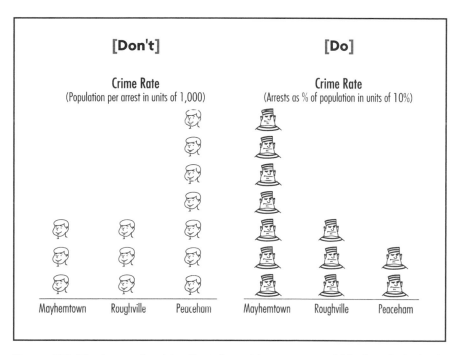

Figure 5.7. The icons should reflect the subject matter, which they do in both panels—but the appearance of the pattern is incompatible with the message in another way: "More" is seen as "more"—so longer bars or greater numbers of icons should specify larger amounts of the relevant substance or more frequent occurrences of the relevant event. In "Don't," greater numbers of icons actually indicate a lower crime rate! Do not convey "less" by "more."

6. Ensure that pictures used to illustrate measured entities depict those entities.

Pictures used to convey quantities either should depict the entities being represented, as in "Do" of Figure 5.8, or should have conventional symbolic interpretations that label those entities (such using an icon of an envelope for a post office or a donkey for the Democratic party).

7. Compare extents at the same orientation.

The "Don't" version of Figure 5.9 immediately demonstrates why this recommendation is a good idea: It is much harder to derive a relationship of quantities among the three elements when there is no common baseline and we must assess the absolute value of each in isolation, remember it, and compare it with the others. And, to make matters worse, our visual systems fall prey to an illusion that makes the same extent seem longer when it's vertical than when it's horizontal.

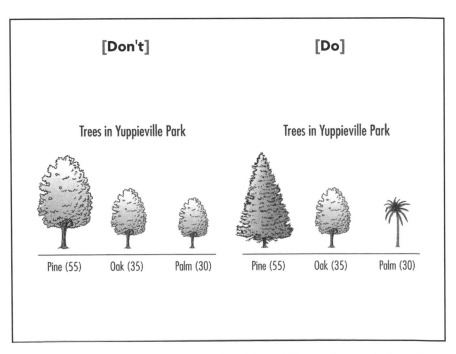

Figure 5.8. Pictures in a visual table should provide another kind of label and should not interfere with the interpretation of the display.

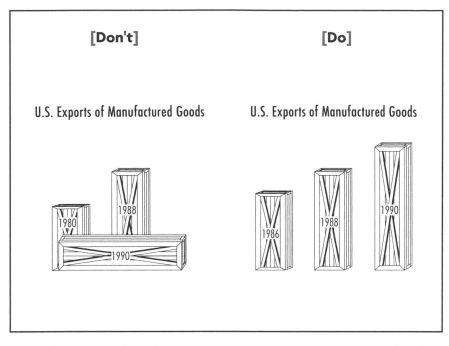

Figure 5.9. It is much easier to compare extents at the same orientation than at different orientations.

8.   Don't vary height and width to specify separate variables.

A designer might use rectangular objects to present seasonal totals for new accounts opened at a bank. The height of each rectangle would indicate the number of accounts that were opened during that particular season; the width, the average amount deposited in such accounts; and the third variable, the area, would indicate the total revenue for each season. This scheme is shown in "Don't" of Figure 5.10. The problem: the audience members will see a rectangle—not height, width, and area as distinct elements.

Line Graphs: 11 Guidelines for Going in the Right Direction

Line graphs and bar graphs are the most common ways to illustrate quantitative information. This section describes when line graphs are more appropriate and summarizes recommendations for making effective line graphs.

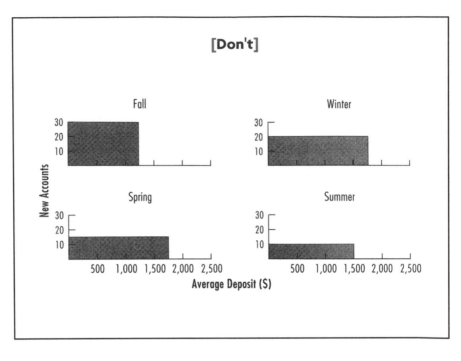

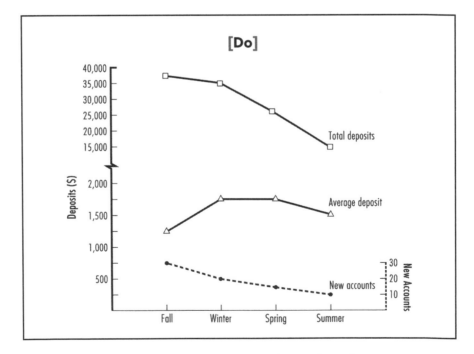

Figure 5.10. The line graph clearly indicates the number of new accounts, the average deposit, and the total deposits per season, as well as the relations among these measures. The same information is embedded in the four panels above, but considerable effort is required to decode it. We perceive height and width as specifying an area, not as separate variables.

1. Use a line graph if the X axis specifies a continuous scale.

The continuous rise and fall of a line is psychologically compatible with a scale that specifies the amounts along a continuous measurement scale. The yearly pattern of a young man's fancy is more clearly perceived from "Do" than from "Don't" in Figure 5.11.

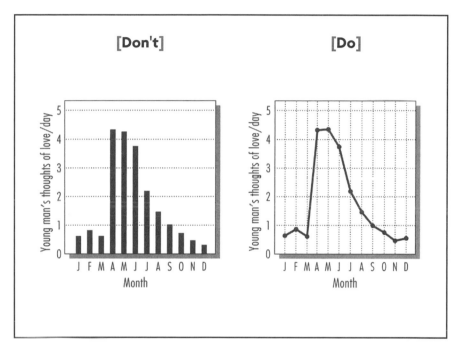

Figure 5.11. The continuous variation of a line is compatible with the continuous variation of time; if you want the viewer to note precise point values, put dots or symbols along the line.

2. Use a line graph to display trends.

The rise and fall of a line creates a shape, which we easily interpret as a trend—up, down, or a period of growth mixed with periods of contraction.

3. In general, use a line graph to display interactions.

One of the reasons it is so difficult to predict real-world events is that multiple variables interact, in a statistical sense: By "interact" I don't mean that two (or more) things have a personal relationship or that one necessarily changes another directly. Rather, I mean that the effects of one variable can be understood only in the context of at least one other. When describing an interaction, you would say that the effects of X depend on the value of Y. For instance, the difference between the average temperature in June and January depends on whether you are in New York or Sydney. This interaction, between month and hemisphere, reflects the dependence of the value of one variable on the value of the other.

- If there is little chance that audience members will improperly infer a continuous scale along the X axis, then a line graph is a good way to convey interactions even if the X axis specifies rankings (not actual intervals) or even names, not amounts at all. But if a line graph would incorrectly imply a continuous scale on the X axis, use a bar graph.
- Except when a line graph would be misleading, avoid using a bar graph to illustrate interactions. In order to see bars as unified patterns that convey interactions, the viewer must mentally connect the ends of the bars, expending time and effort.

Example: Most experienced graph readers can immediately recognize that crossing lines indicate an interaction whereas parallel lines do not.

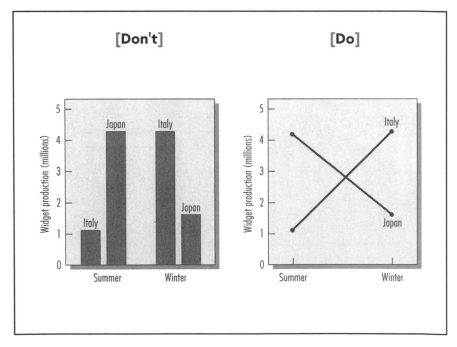

Figure 5.12. Experienced graph readers can interpret typical patterns of lines at a glance. Hence, it is good—especially in a presentation when viewers may not have much time to decode a display—to make use of familiar patterns to convey interactions.

4.   Don't use a line graph to show point values.

If you use a line graph to show specific values, the audience members must locate and perceptually isolate a point along a line and note its height along the Y axis (Figure 5.13). This process violates the Principle of Limited Capacity; it requires the audience to work to understand you. According to one aphorism, "Work isn't a task, it's torture" (L. Bracken, http://deoxy.org/aaw.htm). Why make your audience work any harder than they have to?

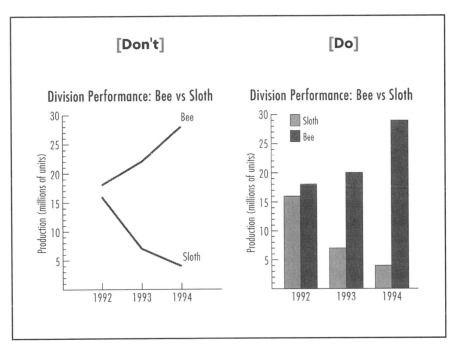

Figure 5.13. The heights of bars define specific points, whereas lines specify continuous variations. It is more difficult perceptually to break up a line into points than to detect the tops of bars.

5.   Ensure that the X and Y axes are clearly identifiable and appropriately labeled.

The viewer should immediately be oriented to the X axis (which typically has values of what is varied or selected to be assessed) and the Y axis (which typically has values of what is measured). I was impressed by the following joke, not because it's funny—but because I've literally seen this happen! "The experimentalist comes running excitedly into the theorist's office, waving a graph taken off his latest experiment. 'Hmmm,' says the theorist, 'That's exactly where you'd expect to see that peak. Here's the reason (long logical explanation follows).' In the middle of it, the experimentalist says 'Wait a minute,' studies the chart for a second, and says, `Oops, this is upside down.' He fixes it. `Hmmm,' says the theorist, `you'd expect to see a dip in exactly that position. Here's the reason . . .' " (www.physlink. com/Fun/Jokes.cfm) Avoid such embarrassing moments by labeling the graph appropriately!

6.   Vary the salience of lines to indicate relative importance.

Viewers will notice the most salient line first and interpret it as the most important. If you are looking at all three networks' morning shows and comparing their ratings, the graph on the left of Figure 5.14 is the style you want. But if your subject is NBC's "Today" and you want to emphasize that show's ratings against the other two shows in the field, the one on the right better illustrates your focus.

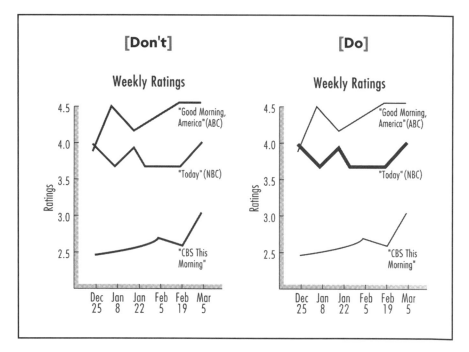

Figure 5.14. If the focus is on NBC, the graph on the right is preferable; the increased salience of the line for NBC immediately draws the viewer's attention.

7.   Ensure that crossing or nearby lines are discriminable.

When lines are nearby or cross often, special care must be taken to ensure that they are discriminable. You can increase discriminability by

- using different colors;
- using dashed lines (and varying the dashes);
- in either case, making sure that the salience of the lines does not vary arbitrarily.

8. Ensure that dashes in lines differ by at least 2 to 1.

To be immediately discriminable from one another, dashed lines should differ in elements per inch in a ratio of at least 2 to 1 (this recommendation follows from the Principle of Perceptual Organization, specifically the aspect of Input Channels, explained in the Appendix). For example, if one line has 4 dashes to the inch, another line at least should have no more than 2 or 8 dashes to the inch.

9. If lines connect discrete points, make the points at least twice as thick as the line.

Some line graphs include dots or symbols that mark specific values on the X axis. In order to be easily discriminated from the line, the dots or symbols should be at least twice as thick as the line (Figure 5.15).

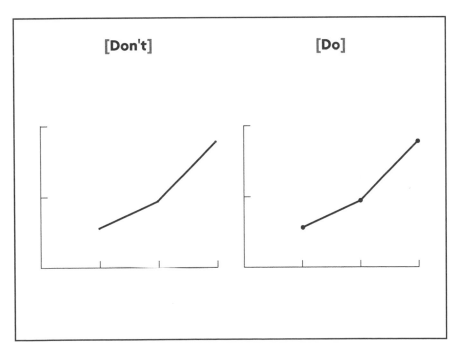

Figure 5.15. The points on the lines are especially important and should be emphasized by discriminable dots.

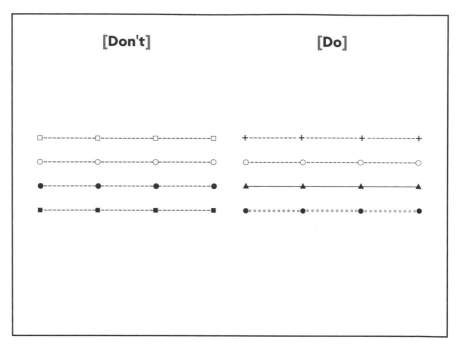

Figure 5.16. Studies have shown that the four lines and symbols on the right are highly discriminable.

10.   Use discriminable symbols for points connected by different lines.

When lines are nearby or cross often, you can enhance discriminability by using visually distinct symbols for important points—either in conjunction with different dashed or colored lines or with solid lines.

Example: Plus signs, Xs, open circles, and filled triangles remain distinct even when reduced to relatively small sizes (Figure 5.16). However, ensure that the difference between filled and unfilled versions of the same element are easy to discern even when the graph is projected onto a screen.

11.   Use an inner grid when precise values are important.

For all variants of line and bar graphs, include an inner grid if you want the audience to be able to extract one or more specific values, which can be read off the Y axis more easily if one can trace along grid lines. Especially with line graphs, insert heavier grid lines at regular intervals, which will help the viewer track from a point on the line to the axes (Figure 5.17).

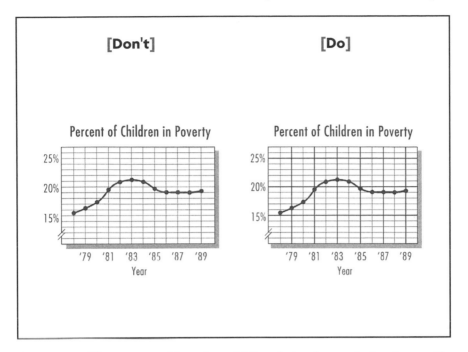

Figure 5.17. The staggered heavier grid lines help viewers to locate specific values on the axes for specific data points.

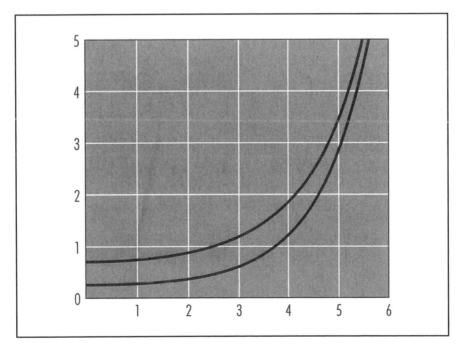

Figure 5.18. Without an inner grid, it is almost impossible to tell that the lines have the same difference in value on the Y axis over the 2 and 5 values on the X axis.

Example: The line graph in Figure 5.18 illustrates a special case in which grid lines are particularly helpful. Look at the vertical difference between the lines over 5 and those over 2; which difference looks larger? In fact, they are the same distance apart, as you will see if you use the grid lines to compare the two differences. Our visual system tends to see the minimal distance between the lines, not their difference in height. Grid lines help the eye to focus on the vertical extent itself.

Bar Graphs: 10 Pillars to Build On

In this section we consider when to use bar graphs and crucial factors to keep in mind when presenting them.

1.   Use a bar graph to illustrate differences between specific point values.

The ends of the bars in bar graphs specify particular values. If you want to contrast the measurements of a set of entities, use a bar graph.

2.   Don't use a bar graph to illustrate trends.

To see a trend in a bar graph, viewers must mentally connect the tops of the bars. Why make them expend the effort? If showing trends is your goal, show them a line graph.

3.   Use a bar graph if more than two values are on an X axis that does not show a continuous scale.

Look at the "Don't" version of Figure 5.19, in which the line makes it appear as if the income for consulting partners is accelerating rapidly. This visual impression is less striking in "Do". If the intervals of space along the X axis don't specify a continuously varying scale, a line will give a misleading impression of a trend. However, as noted earlier, if you want to show an interaction, consider using a line graph even in this situation. Your audience can quickly see that lines cross or diverge, but will need to work harder to see relations among sets of bars.

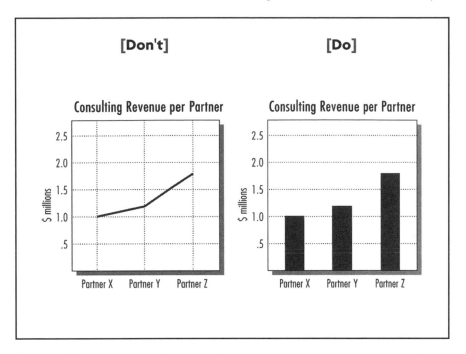

Figure 5.19. A line graph for these data inappropriately suggests a rapid rise along a continuous variation.

4.   Use a horizontal bar graph if the labels are too long to fit under a vertical bar graph.

If a vertical bar graph requires novel abbreviations, audience members may receive less information than they need in order to decipher the material effortlessly.

As noted for line graphs, always be sure that the axes are clearly identifiable and clearly labeled. This is especially important for horizontal bar graphs, which are less common than vertical ones. The viewer should know immediately where to find the independent variable (things that are varied or selected to be assessed) and the dependent variable (the measurement values).

5.   Don't use mixed bar/line displays to show interactions.

As is evident in "Don't" of Figure 5.20, it is more difficult to see interactions if a mixed display is used because bars and lines don't group to form simple patterns; to help the audience grasp interactions, use multiple lines.

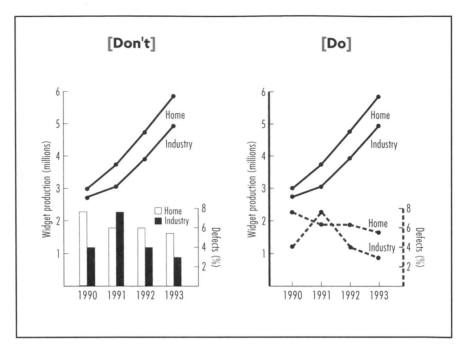

Figure 5.20. The trend toward decreasing numbers of defects with increasing production, especially for the industrial widget, is not immediately evident from the mixed line/bar display; the visual system more easily groups different lines into a pattern than it groups lines and bars.

6. Mark corresponding bars in the same way.

Mark the corresponding bars in each cluster the same way so that they are grouped appropriately (exploiting the grouping law of similarity), as in "Do". Try to compare the performance of the two brands of Coca-Cola in 1989 from the "Don't" graph in Figure 5.21. This is not as easy as it should be because, in a misplaced attempt at variety in the way the bars are shaded, the designer used different shadings for corresponding elements.

7. Arrange corresponding bars in the same way.

Say you want to graph numbers of young and old men and women voters for each of two counties. The demographic groups for each county would be on the X axis, and 4 bars, one for each of the groups (young men, old men, young women, old women) would be presented. The demographic groups could be indicated by different shading. The order of the bars for voter groups should be the same for each county, as in "Do" in Figure 5.22. If it isn't, the audience members will waste time trying to make comparisons and wondering why the order differs.

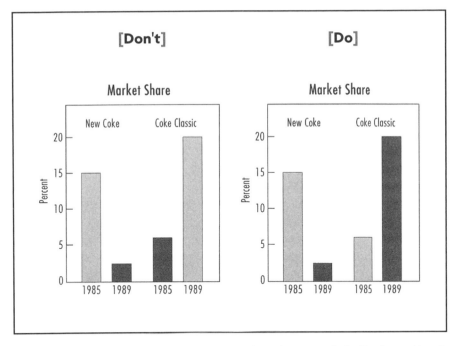

Figure 5.21. Inconsistent marking groups bars improperly in Don't, making it harder to compare corresponding elements.

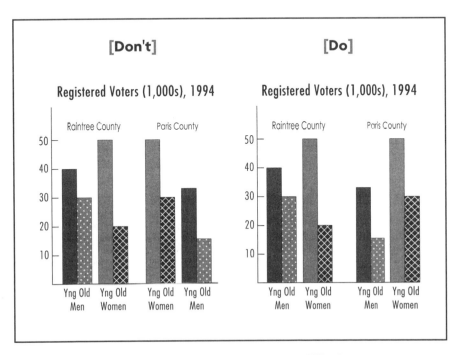

Figure 5.22. A gratuitous change of order makes it difficult to compare corresponding bars.

8. Don't vary the salience of individual bars arbitrarily.

Unless the emphasis is intentional, no bar should stand out from the others as happens in "Do" in Figure 5.23; if it does, the difference in salience will lead the audience to notice it first, and assume that it is more important than the other bars in the display.

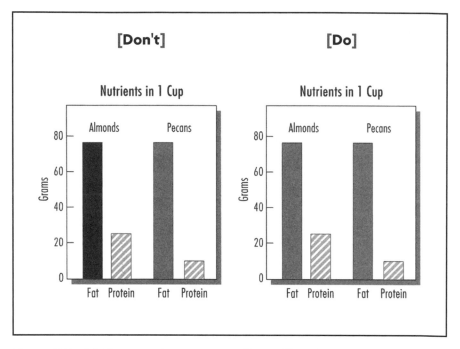

Figure 5.23. Making one element very salient will put it at the center of attention. If you want to emphasize that element, this is appropriate; but if you are simply trying to provide visual variety, as here, it is likely to confuse the audience.

9. Leave space between bar clusters.

Notice in Figure 5.24 how much easier it is to compare the market shares in 1985 for the three brands in "Don't" versus "Do". Group bar clusters over each appropriate location on the X axis and leave extra space between the clusters. As a rule of thumb, the space between clusters should be about as wide as two bars (this advice follows from the Principle of Perceptual Organization, specifically the aspect of Input Channels; see the Appendix).

10. Avoid extending bars beyond the end of the scale.

Don't make bars extend over the top of the Y axis, as in "Don't" in Figure 5.25 (or to the right of the X axis, in a horizontal bar graph) if

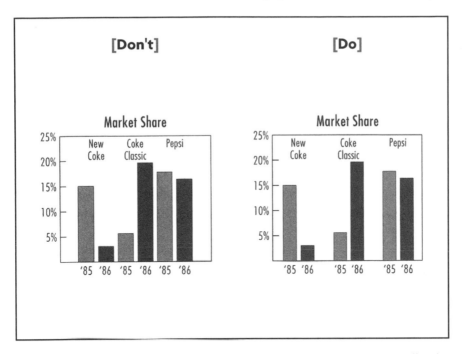

Figure 5.24. Six perceptual units are too many to apprehend immediately; proper grouping not only makes the display easier to take in but also helps to group the bars with their labels.

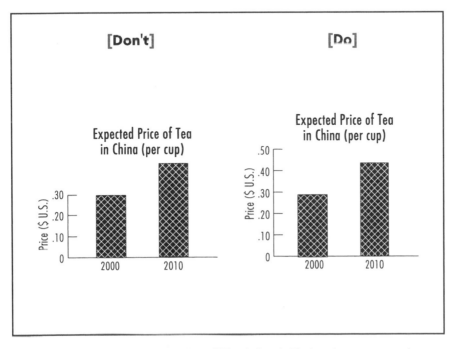

Figure 5.25. If the Y axis is too short ("Don't," at left), the viewer cannot immediately estimate the price of tea in 2010.

the viewers are supposed to be able to extract specific point values; mentally continuing the axis and its scale requires effort. However, if the point of the display is not to show specific values but only to indicate that, say, housing prices have shot through the roof, then you would just be adding extraneous details by including tick marks, labels on the Y axis, and so on. Some of the most effective graphs in *Time* magazine have tall bars that extend into the text, driving home the point that some trend has exploded beyond its usual boundaries.

Step Graphs: 4 Ways to Step Up

A step graph is a step-like line that can be thought of as formed by the tops of bars that have been pushed together.

1.   Use a step graph to illustrate a trend among more than two entities that vary along a noncontinuous scale.

A step graph is useful if the audience members are supposed to notice relative changes over three or more values on the X axis but these values don't vary continuously and using lines would suggest inappropriate trends. Pushing the bars together creates a pattern that may allow the viewer to take in a trend at a glance.

- One drawback to these displays is that a bit more effort is required to isolate individual point values, and so a bar graph (where spaces between the bars isolate the individual bars, which convey point values) is more appropriate if this emphasis is your goal.
- Another drawback is that—depending on the data being plotted— patterns sometimes can be difficult to see. If this occurs, consider using a line graph (and in your presentation, explicitly point out the ways in which this graph may be misleading, but explain why it is good for showing the relevant interaction).

2.   If the lines cross, don't include two or more lines in a step graph.

From the "Don't" graph in Figure 5.26 it is almost impossible to tell the percentage of automobile sales for the different countries. In these situations, present the data in separate panels, as shown in "Do". Such displays can illustrate different trends effectively, but do not illustrate interactions well.

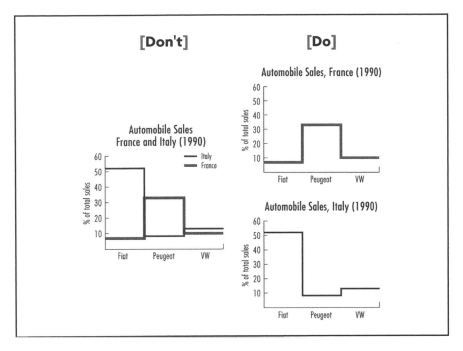

Figure 5.26. A combined step graph is difficult to read and easily mistaken as illustrating a cumulative total.

3.   Make the steps of equal width.

In which version of the graph in Figure 5.27 does U.S. investment in Germany look more important? The reader will mistakenly perceive a wider step as representing a greater amount, even if that step is the same height as another, narrower step. Make sure the steps are of equal width, not drawn as in "Don't".

4.   Fill the area under the line with a single pattern or color.

The primary virtue of step graphs is that they produce patterns that indicate specific trends. As is evident in "Do," if the area under the line is filled with a color or texture that is different from the background, the grouping law of similarity (as summarized in the Appendix) will lead the viewer to see that area as a single shape, facilitating recognition of a trend. But only a single color or texture should be used; otherwise, the impression of a single region will be disrupted.

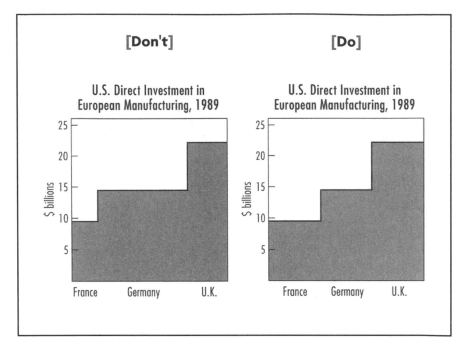

Figure 5.27. Making one step wider than the others gives it unequal importance.

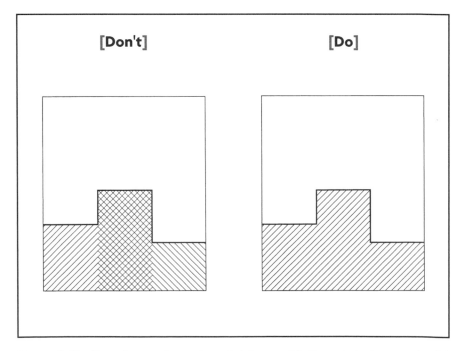

Figure 5.28. The shape of a series of rising and falling steps is meaningful and should not be disrupted.

Scatterplots: Ways to Avoid Scattershot

A scatterplot can look like random holes in a barn door or an army of ants marching in the same direction. This format uses the same sort of axes used in line and bar graphs, but now individual points are plotted rather than lines or bars.

1.   Use a scatterplot to convey an overall impression of the relation between two variables.

Scatterplots are appropriate if you want audience members to obtain only an overall impression of the relation between two variables and you want the audience to have a sense of the variability of the relation between the variables.

Example: If the heights and weights of 100 people are plotted, viewers will see a cloud drifting up toward the right, indicating that the two variables are positively correlated. Moreover, viewers also can see that this correlation is not perfect; some very tall people are skinny, and some short ones rotund.

Don't include a grid, as in "Don't" in Figure 5.29; the point is to convey an overall trend, not individual values. Scatterplots often include far more points than can be grouped and seen as individuals; therefore, they are not a good idea if audience members are supposed to discern specific point values (use a table instead but present only the truly important values; otherwise you will overwhelm the viewers).

2.   Avoid illustrating pairs of measurements for more than one category in a scatterplot.

Don't plot the pairs of measurements (such as the heights and weights) of different categories, such as Northerners and Southerners or Americans and Europeans, with different symbols for the points in the same scatterplot; the points will be intermixed and very difficult to discriminate. The only exceptions to this recommendation occur if you want to show that:

- data from two categories are intimately related (and so the fact that the points cannot be distinguished is itself compatible with the message being conveyed);
- data from two categories are clearly distinct (as evident when the clouds formed by different sets of points can be easily distinguished because they are in different parts of the display).

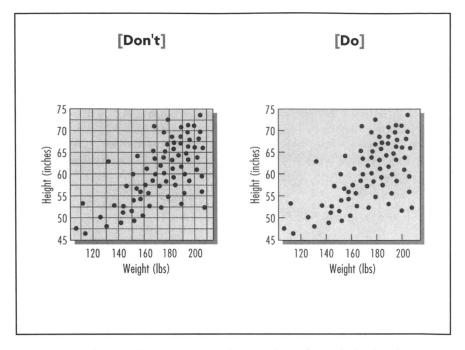

Figure 5.29. Scatterplots convey an impression of trends in the data; they generally are not well suited for conveying values of individual data points, and an inner grid is usually a distraction.

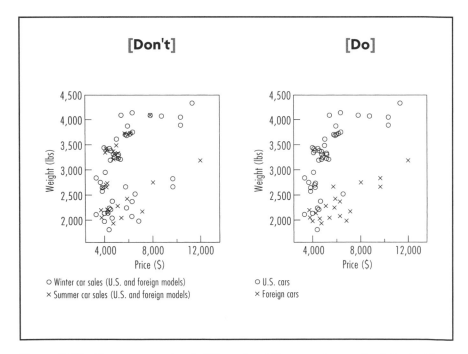

Figure 5.30. Measurements of different entities can be easily detected in a scatterplot only if their symbols occupy different parts of the display.

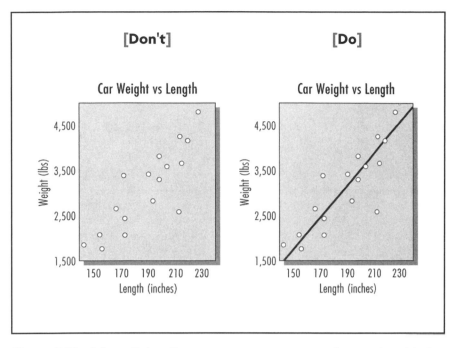

Figure 5.31. A best-fitting line serves as a summary of a trend and helps viewers to see the strength of the correlation between two variables.

3. Fit a line through a scatterplot to show how closely two variables are related.

In many cases, scatterplots are used to illustrate a trend, which can be summarized effectively by a line. Unlike the line in a line graph, this "fitted" line does not connect up sets of points. Rather, it falls through the "center"—the most densely populated area—of the cloud of points. The most popular way to fit such a line requires finding the location that minimizes the average distance of the points to the line (which is known as the "method of least squares").

Multiple Panels

When should you divide the data up and display it in separate panels?

1. Avoid presenting more than four perceptual units in one panel.

Our friend the *Rule of Four* applies here again: If at all possible, present no more than four bars or clusters of bars in a single panel. If there are more than four bars over each point on the X axis, or more than four groups of lines, find a way to divide the data into subsets and graph each subset in a separate panel (Figure 5.32).

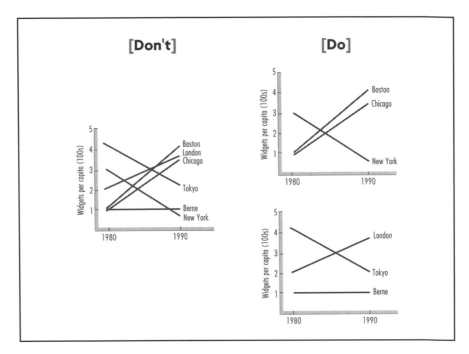

Figure 5.32. A display containing more than four perceptual units cannot be apprehended in a glance. Break such displays into separate panels.

2. Use multiple panels to highlight specific comparisons.

It is easier to compare material within a panel than across panels, so ensure that the data are organized to help the audience make the most important comparisons (Figure 5.33).

3. Graph different types of data in a single display only if they are strongly related and must be compared.

As a rule, don't graph different types of data in the same display; in most cases, graph the different data in separate panels of a multipanel

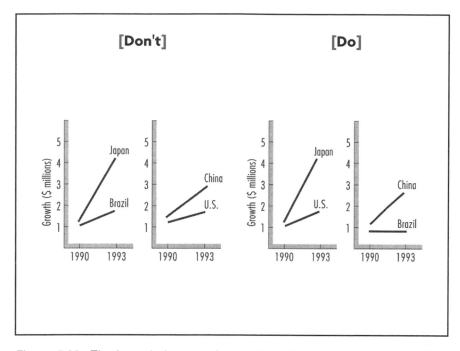

Figure 5.33. The intended comparisons—here, between two countries that have been industrialized for a long time and two emerging nations—are facilitated by appropriate grouping.

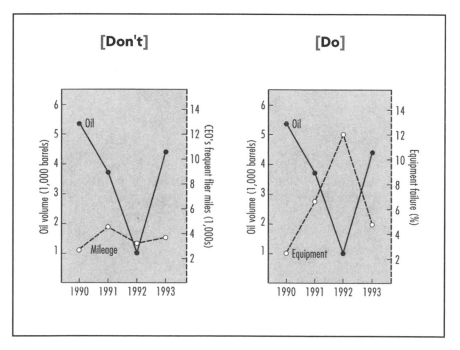

Figure 5.34. Plotting two related variables together can reveal useful information, such as the impact of equipment failure on the amount of oil that was pumped.

display. Graphing two types of measurements in the same display forces the audience to keep track of which bars or lines go with which scales, taxing their limited processing capacity.

The only exception to this recommendation occurs when the measured variables are intimately related and their interrelations are critical to the message being conveyed; in this situation, plotting the data in the same display allows the laws of perceptual grouping to organize them into a single pattern.

> **Example:** The volume of oil pumped and the failure rate of a piece of pumping equipment are probably connected, and it makes sense to graph these two sets of measurements in one display, as in "Do" in Figure 5.34. On the other hand, oil volume and the CEO's frequent-flier mileage ("Don't") are not as immediately related, and the graph is not particularly helpful.

From the Principles to the Point

All of these recommendations stem from the eight psychological principles. If you understand the principles and how to apply them, graph design will become simple and natural. I again summarize each principle and note which ones contributed primarily to each of the major recommendations offered earlier in the chapter.

Principle of Relevance: Communication is most effective when neither too much nor too little information is presented. (We understand and remember a message more easily when the right amount of detail is used to make the point.)

- Present data needed for a specific purpose.
- Graph different types of data in a single display only if they are highly related and must be compared.

Principle of Appropriate Knowledge: Communication requires prior knowledge of pertinent concepts, jargon, and symbols. (We understand and remember a message more easily if it connects to what we already know.)

- Use concepts and display formats that are familiar to the audience.

Principle of Salience: Attention is drawn to large perceptible differences. (Big relative differences grab attention.)

- Use an exploded pie to emphasize a small proportion of parts.
- Explode a maximum of 25 percent of the wedges.
- Vary the salience of lines to indicate relative importance.
- Don't vary the salience of individual bars arbitrarily.

Principle of Discriminability: Two properties must differ by a large enough proportion or they will not be distinguished. (We need contrast to distinguish shapes, colors, or positions from each other and from the background.)

- Ensure that crossing or nearby lines are discriminable.
- Use discriminable symbols for points connected by different lines.
- Avoid illustrating pairs of measurements with different types of points for more than one category in a scatterplot.

Principle of Perceptual Organization: People automatically group elements into units, which they then attend to and remember. (These groups are easier to see and remember than the isolated components would be.)

- Compare extents at the same orientation.
- Don't vary height and width to specify separate variables.
- Ensure that dashes in lines differ by at least 2 to 1.
- If lines connect discrete points, make the points at least twice as thick as the line.
- Don't use mixed bar/line displays to show interactions.
- Leave space between bar clusters.
- Avoid extending bars beyond the end of the scale.
- Use an inner grid when precise values are important.
- Fill the area under the line in a step graph with a single pattern or color.

Principle of Compatibility: A message is easiest to understand if its form is compatible with its meaning. (For better or worse, the mind tends to judge a book by its cover.)

- Use a graph to illustrate relative amounts.
- Use a pie to convey approximate relative proportions.
- Use a visual table to convey impressions of relative amounts.
- Don't use the area of elements to convey precise quantities.
- Use sets of icons to provide labels or to compare relative amounts.
- Make the appearance of the pattern compatible with what it symbolizes.
- Ensure that pictures used to illustrate measured entities depict those entities.

- Use a line graph if the X axis specifies a continuous scale.
- Use a line graph to display trends.
- Use a line graph to display interactions over two entities on the X axis.
- Use a bar graph to illustrate differences between specific point values.
- Use a bar graph if more than two values are on an X axis that does not specify a continuous scale.
- Use a step graph to illustrate a trend among more than two entities that vary along a noncontinuous scale.
- Use a scatterplot to convey an overall impression of the relationship between two variables.

Principle of Informative Changes: People expect changes in properties to carry information. (And we expect every necessary piece of information to be indicated by a change in a perceptible property.)

- Label wedges of pie graphs if precise values are important.
- Ensure that the X and Y axes are clearly identifiable and appropriately labeled.
- Provide labels to specify relevant precise amounts.
- Use a horizontal bar graph if the labels are too long to fit under a vertical display.
- Mark corresponding bars in the same way.
- Arrange corresponding bars in the same way.
- Make steps in step graphs equal width.
- Fit a line through a scatterplot to show how closely two variables are related.

Principle of Capacity Limitations: People have a limited capacity to retain and to process information, and so will not understand a message if too much information must be retained or processed. (From a communicative point of view, less can be more!)

- Arrange wedges of pie graphs in a simple progression.
- Don't use a line graph to show point values.
- Don't use a bar graph to illustrate trends.
- If proportions vary greatly, don't use multiple pies to compare corresponding parts.
- Avoid presenting more than four perceptual units in one panel.
- Use multiple panels to highlight specific comparisons.

Communicating Qualitative Information: Charts, Diagrams, Maps, Photographs, and Clipart

6

PowerPoint Jedi use their skills with PowerPoint to make difficult concepts clear. Me, I'm a PowerPoint Sith. I use my PowerPoint skills to confuse and obfuscate. If my boss doesn't have a glazed look of bewilderment, then the brief isn't complete. Embrace the dark side.

—Mike Aitken (www.nbc-links.com/powerpoint.html)

If a perverse impulse leads you to want to confuse and obfuscate, it's easy to succeed. I've already mentioned a common technique, which is to pack immense amounts of text on every slide (using a tiny, barely discriminable font), from which you read random samples in a soft monotone. Even insomniacs will be overcome by such treatment.

Another sure-fire way to mow down an audience is to keep the material extremely abstract, so that it sounds good but the audience won't really know what you are talking about. Yet another approach that will sow bewilderment and confusion is to make claims that simply don't reflect reality—and assert them with great confidence. And you can use graphics that are meaningless or that have little bearing on your message; they might look very attractive, and distract the audience from your lack of clarity.

On the other hand, if your goal is to be clear and to the point, and to present a compelling case for your point of view, then you should present concrete evidence for your claims, which are presented in a logical sequence. To keep the audience's interest and attention, you need variety. Present graphics and sound to illustrate what you say—show and tell. This will not only make your presentation more interesting but will also make the material more comprehensible and will root what you say in reality.

The eight psychological principles apply to all communication graphics, including ones that convey qualitative information:

- *Charts* specify qualitative relationships among entities; family trees and flowcharts are charts.
- *Diagrams* are schematic pictures of objects or events that rely on conventionally defined symbols (such as arrows to indicate forces); "exploded" diagrams that show how parts of an object fit together and illustrations of football plays are diagrams.
- *Maps* present both qualitative and quantitative information; they not only portray geographical features, but also implicitly specify distances among locations, a quantitative variable.
- *Photographs and Clipart,* where the latter includes cartoons and drawings that illustrate people, ideas, or situations. These illustrations can be found online and easily pasted onto a slide (provided that they are in the public domain or proper copyright permissions are obtained; When in doubt, consult your lawyer!).

I begin with general recommendations, then turn to specific recommendations for each type of display.

General Recommendations for Charts, Diagrams, Maps, Photographs, and Clipart

The following recommendations apply to all of the types of graphics discussed in this chapter.

1.   **Include only graphics that help you make your point.**

Decorations are distracting and may undermine your credibility if they seem cute or frivolous. Remember: A PowerPoint presentation should have a point!

2.   **Include only *the parts of* graphics that help you make your point.**

Even when the graphic is appropriate, parts of it may not be. Include only material that is directly relevant to the specific point you are making at any given time. A diagram meant to show the driver's controls in an automobile may not be helpful to the viewer if many other automotive systems also are shown, as in "Don't" in Figure 6.1.

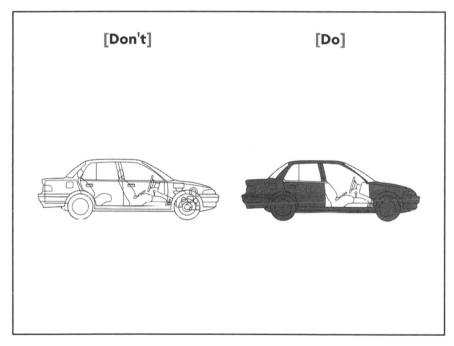

Figure 6.1. A diagram intended to show the driver's position relative to key controls is easier to read if the irrelevant components are eliminated and the relevant ones are highlighted.

3.   **Use symbols, concepts, and jargon that are familiar to the audience members.**

Certain disciplines—electronics, genetics, and linguistics, to name a few—use specific specialized symbols, which should be used when appropriate. Depending on context, however, the same symbol may have different meanings. For instance, an arrow may indicate parts to be matched, direction of force, or movement.

- If you even suspect that your audience may be in doubt about the meanings of the symbols you are using, state those meanings explicitly.

  Example: When describing a flowchart, indicate whether different shapes—such as squares and diamonds—have different meanings (such as an operation versus a decision/branching point).

- Also be sure that the audience is comfortable with the concepts and jargon you use. If you have any doubt, define the terms.

  Example: Instead of simply saying "a branching point" when describing a flowchart, say "A branching point, where a decision is made about the next sequence of steps to take."

4. Ensure that all aspects of the graphic are clearly discriminable from the background.

The graphic must have enough contrast with the background to be visible throughout the room and must be large enough to be legible even from the back row.

5. Change visual or auditory characteristics only to signal a change in information.

The Principle of Informative Changes applies to all types of graphics.

  Example: Clipart or a photograph alerts the audience to pay attention to a new idea or claim; if nothing is new, don't introduce a new piece of Clipart or a photo.

6. Organize the components of complex displays.

A graphic can effectively convey a complex set of qualitative relations if the complexity doesn't visually overwhelm the relations depicted.

To avoid producing a tangled web or overwhelming pastiche, divide different aspects of the display into separate perceptual units (see Figure 6.2). These units can be defined by:

- Similar shapes
- Similar colors
- Similar shadings
- Similar sizes
- Similar line weights
- A line or arrow that links objects
- Nearby locations, which are clearly distinct from other clusters

Finally, you can also produce groups simply by presenting a subset of the material at a time, and build up the whole display over the course of a series of slides.

In "Do" in Figure 6.2, the phases of the data collection and evaluation process are distinguished from the decision processes. Similarly, many flowcharts use diamond shapes when a decision is made, squares when a process occurs, and circles when input or output occurs.

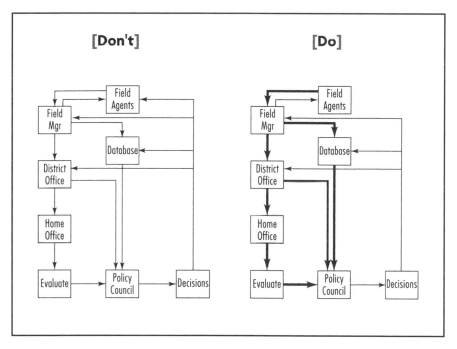

Figure 6.2. A complex chart can be sorted out relatively easily if it is visually organized into components.

7. Respect the *Rule of Four*: Don't expect viewers to attend to more than four perceptual units on a slide.

If you want viewers to pay attention to more than four objects in your graphic, devise a way to present them as groups (using the variables noted in the previous recommendation), so that there are no more than four groups. The crucial limiting factor is the number of perceptual units (i.e., groups), not the actual number of objects.

How can you tell how many perceptual units are present? Fortunately, studies have shown that people are remarkably accurate and consistent at drawing lines around the parts of a displayed object or scene, which correspond well to the perceptual units. Thus, you need only consider where you would draw lines between parts or groups of objects, and you'll have a good sense of how many units there are.

8. Use animation and vary salience to guide the audience through the display.

If the point of the graphic requires the audience to grasp a sequence of events, use animation to illustrate that sequence. If you need to vary the speed of animation, use the "custom animation" feature (under the Slide Show menu item, at least in my current version of the program), and put a set of objects on a single slide, defining the animation values for each. Alternatively, make a series of slides, like frames in a film, and use the "slide transition" feature to specify how long each one is visible (but in this case you will need to experiment with the number of frames and exposures in order to produce acceptable motion). If the display does not lend itself to movement, vary salience—by changing the display over time—to guide the viewers' attention.

Example: By systematically changing the colors of specific states of the United States in a series of slides, you could illustrate the course of the western expansion during the 18th and 19th centuries.

9. Use multiple panels to highlight specific comparisons.

If your initial display is too complicated, and you cannot easily group the elements into 4 or fewer perceptual units (as noted above), break the display into separate panels.

- Decide which units are most closely interacting (e.g., in a flowchart) or are most closely related (e.g., adjacent territories in a map), and present them together.
- To provide the overall context, gray out the rest of the display.
- If the display is so large or complex that individual components cannot be clearly seen, "zoom in" on one part at a time. Provide a

"thumbnail sketch" at the upper right, showing (e.g., with a red square) the relative location of the current material within the context of the whole. In such cases work through the display systematically, to help viewers integrate each portion into the whole.

Charts: 6 Pointers

Charts can make complex sets of information clear at a glance, or can make complex information seem even more complex. For instance, consider one chart that was created in the wake of Hurricane Katrina. This hurricane was no laughing matter, nor was the feeble response of the Federal Emergency Management Agency (FEMA). Nevertheless, Jon Stewart, the host of the *Daily Show* (broadcast on Comedy Central), couldn't help commenting on a chart released by FEMA (during the week of 26 September 2005), Figure 6.3. He said: "What should FEMA have done? Perhaps the answer can be found on their website. . . . This chart [shown below], clearly depicting the agency's responsibilities in the event of a disaster. . . . It begins with a response to a disaster, leads to recovery, mitigation, risk reduction, prevention, preparedness . . . (dramatic pause) and

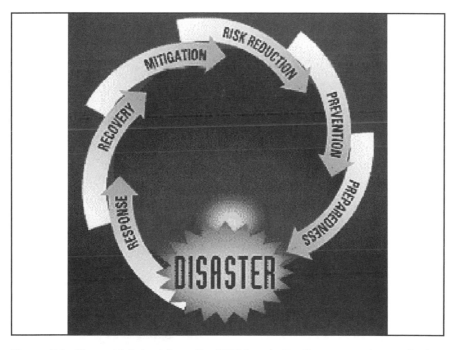

Figure 6.3. The actual chart from the FEMA website. Can you understand what it means?

ends up BACK IN DISASTER! . . . In truth, FEMA did exactly what they *said* they were going to do" (http://presentationzen.blogs.com/ presentationzen/2005/10/fema_chart_beco.html).

Charts are visual displays that arrange information into categories or structures. Usually, lines connect the elements of a chart to indicate structure; but the arrangement of the elements (such as boxes or even just words) on the screen may be enough to show the relationship clearly. The FEMA Chart? The bad news is that it inadvertently shows how disasters beget disasters. Moreover, according to their website, their cycle actually begins with (not ends with, as shown here), "Preparedness" and ends with "Response," but this still doesn't fit with the use of arrows—which might suggest that the "Response" leads to the disaster! The good news is that it's almost impossible to read this chart (notice how hard it is to read all upper case, especially when the words are at odd angles and even upside down).

1.   Use a chart to convey overall organizational structure.

Using a chart to illustrate the structure of an object, organization, or event takes advantage of the Principle of Compatibility. Relationships such as "is a member of," "follows," "works for," and "is descended from" can be illustrated clearly by the spatial relations of the entities in the display.

2.   Use a chart to illustrate sequences of steps over time.

The PowerPoint program lets you show even complex sequences of events by building up a chart, a part at a time.

3.   Use a list to convey one relation among several entities.

The alternative to a chart is a list, which is preferable if only a single relation and four or fewer entities need be considered.

Example: A simple list can effectively convey a simple organization:

Company Divisions
- Consulting
- Publishing

People can read such a list faster than they can decipher a chart, and a short list will tax short-term memory less than would a multi-element display. However, if you want the viewers to compare numerous different combinations of entities (such as the relations between various managers and their superiors in the company), a chart is better than a list. In the wise words of Albert Einstein, "Everything should be made as simple as possible, but not one bit simpler."

4. Show more inclusive categories higher in the display.

Say that the problem is to show how the Mega Corporation breaks down into separate divisions. Place the larger entities higher in a chart with the entities that are contained within the larger entities depicted beneath them.

> **Example:** Mega Corp. has automotive, consumer electronics, and ranching divisions. These would be symbolized in a chart by boxes (or pictures of representative objects) in a row directly beneath the box (or picture) representing the company. Beneath each of these three entities would be boxes or pictures for their components.

5. Use a layout compatible with the subject matter.

A chart detailing the command structure of an organization (Figure 6.4b) should start at the top and work down, as in "Do"; it should not go from left to right.

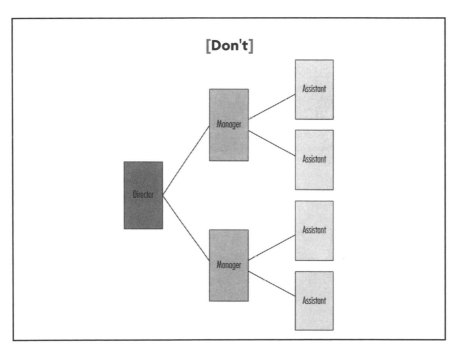

Figure 6.4a. Category inclusion and command structure both correspond to vertical spatial relations because some categories or positions are "over" others; the unfolding of events over time is shown better in a horizontal layout.

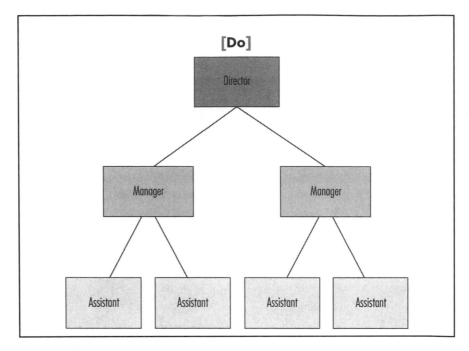

Figure 6.4b.

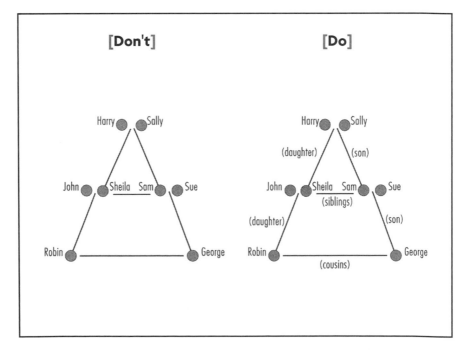

Figure 6.5. Every important piece of information, whether entity or relationship, should be identified in the display.

- All else being equal, respect the convention in Western culture and make a sequence over time proceed from left to right.
- However, respect the specific conventions of your audience. For example, computer programmers have developed a specialized subculture, where flowcharts are often presented from the top down.

6. Identify relationships.

Identify every important piece of information in a display, as in the "Do" version of this family tree. (Figure 6.5).

Diagrams: 8 Recommendations

Diagrams are pictures of objects or events that use both pictorial elements and symbols (such as arrows to show movement) to convey information—to show the wiring in your kitchen, the way the Eiffel Tower sways in a strong wind, or the assembly of your new barbeque. Unlike charts, parts of diagrams must resemble the things they represent.

1. Use a diagram to illustrate the structure of an object or event for a specific purpose.

When designing a diagram to illustrate the structure of an object or event, keep the purpose of the diagram in mind from the outset. If you don't, you may end up including too much or too little material—leaving the viewers frustrated or annoyed.

2. Explode a diagram to emphasize the shapes or spatial relations of individual parts.

If the parts are partially concealed and you want to make their shapes or spatial relations very clear, move parts away from the whole—but be sure to use an arrow or other visual means to indicate clearly where each part belongs.

3. Don't explode an object too widely for easy recognition.

If the parts are exploded in order to show how they fit together, don't expect the viewer to extrapolate or remember precise spatial relations

among parts of a display; the brain processes shape and spatial relations in separate systems and does not easily combine the two very
accurately. In an exploded diagram, show parts near their actual locations on or in the object depicted, as in "Do" in Figure 6.6.

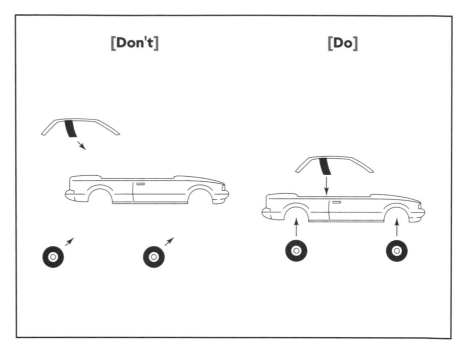

Figure 6.6. If spatial relations are distorted to show components, the distortion should be easy to reintegrate; otherwise, readers will have to expend
effort to see the components in place.

4. Ensure that different components of the diagram are organized into separate perceptual units.

Exploding is not the only way to specify the shapes of parts; different
colors or shading can also be used to individuate parts. If distinct
parts are to be shown, ensure that they are easily identifiable as distinct parts.

5. Use compatible movement when presenting a diagram of a dynamic event.

You can simulate the process of assembling or modifying an object
or tracking a process (such as the effects of a strong wind hitting the
side of a skyscraper) by using animation to add, remove, or modify
parts of a diagram over time.

- Ensure that the order and way in which parts are added, removed, or modified (e.g., shown to bend) mimics the actual order or way in which they would be added, removed, or modified. This technique allows you to discuss each relevant part before turning to the next, and the use of animation will draw the viewers' attention to the next topic of discussion.

6. Choose a point of view in which all critical aspects of the material are visible.

Information that is hidden may as well not exist.

7. Show all parts of static diagrams from the same viewpoint.

The cubists shocked and befuddled their contemporaries by painting objects as if they were seen from multiple points of view simultaneously. At the time, this was a good way to get the attention of the critics and the public, and to lead viewers to consider reality in new ways. But what works well in art (at least for some people) does not necessarily work well in communication graphics. In fact, most people will be confused and have to struggle to understand what you are showing them if you show it from more than a single point of view: The brain assumes that an object is seen from only a single vantage point, and effort will be required to reorganize the display mentally if it is not.

- Similarly, never have one part of the display drawn in two dimensions with a three-dimensional part tacked on to it.

8. Use animation to illustrate three-dimensional structure.

One way to illustrate the structure of a three-dimensional object is to use animation to rotate it in depth. The rotation will be most effective if:

- It is as slow as possible while still revealing the overall structure.
- Four or fewer perceptual units are highlighted (e.g., with a distinctive color).

Example: I've seen many rotating images of the human brain, with colors highlighting specific parts—such as the regions involved in vision. Sometimes the colors come on in sequence, illustrating how the specific brain areas interact. Such information is much easier to grasp when the object appears three dimensional, which it does when rotating.

Maps: 12 Key Considerations

The following is reputed to be an actual transcript of a radio conversation between a Canadian communications officer and a U.S. naval vessel, recorded off the coast of Newfoundland in October 1995:

Americans: Please divert your course 15 degrees to the north to avoid a collision.

Canadians: Recommend you divert YOUR course 15 degrees to the south to avoid a collision.

Americans: This is the Captain of a U.S. Navy ship. I say again, divert your course.

Canadians: No. I say again, you divert your course.

Americans: This is the aircraft carrier USS Lincoln, the second largest ship in the United States' Atlantic fleet! We are accompanied by three destroyers, three cruisers, and numerous support vessels. I demand that you change your course 15 degrees north, that's one-five degrees north, or countermeasures will be undertaken to ensure the safety of this ship!

Canadians: We are a lighthouse. Your call.

If we are to accept this report as gospel (which may be dubious, given that it is posted on the Web both as a joke and as an "actual transcript," as was characterized by the then-president of Duke University, Nannerl O. Keohane, in a speech to the Canadian Club of Ottawa on 28 October 1999, http://canada.usembassy.gov/content/textonly.asp?section=can_usa&document=keohane&subsection1=moreinfo), you could easily fault the participants for their attitudes or communication skills. But in my view the major culprit would probably have been something else: the navigation maps. These maps should have made the location of the lighthouse crystal clear, and should have made it easy to establish where the ships were in relation to the lighthouse.

Maps are drawings that function as pictures of a physical layout. As stylized pictures of a territory, maps provide information about locations and relations among them (usually in terms of relative distances and routes between them). By using conventional markings, they can also provide quantitative information about various locations, such as average temperature, voting patterns, and population distribution.

1. Use a map to show distances of segments or angles between segments of a route.

Use a map if the relative distances between landmarks or angles of turns are important.

2. Use a map if more than one route is possible.

One alternative to a map is a verbal description of a route or territory. However, if you can reach the destination from a number of different starting places or by more than one route between two locations, a map is distinctly more helpful.

3. Use a map to label complex sets of information about a territory.

Maps are also a convenient way to provide various sorts of information about sets of localities; a map allows the viewer to see the relations among different values in many locations.

Example: If population is presented (perhaps by bars standing on particular locations), the viewer can not only see the relation of population to specific landmarks, such as rivers or the sea, but also gain an impression of the pattern of population variations as a whole.

4. Provide neither more nor less detail than required for the point to be made.

If you want to illustrate how to get to the nearest fire station from Harvard Square, it would not be helpful to include every road in the region, as in "Don't" in Figure 6.7. Instead, illustrate the roads that are efficient routes between the two locations, providing enough landmarks that the traveler won't get lost.

• Moreover, if distance per se is not crucial but the sequence of turns is, there is no reason to draw the map to scale. However, if you don't draw the map to scale, indicate when distance has been compressed—such as by using the same sort of truncation marks used to indicate that a Y axis in a graph as been altered (which has the advantage of probably being a familiar symbol to most viewers). However, because some viewers may not be familiar with

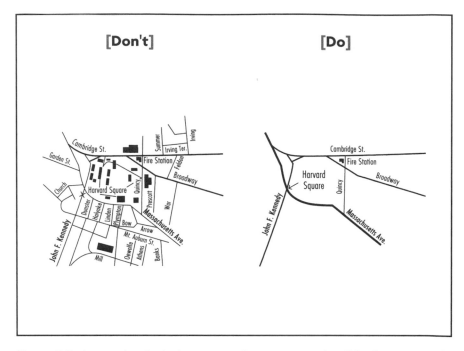

Figure 6.7. A map that includes too much extraneous detail for its purpose is not helpful; to specify the location of the firehouse, only the efficient routes are necessary.

the conventions for indicating truncation, be sure to explain what such symbols mean.

5. Don't vary sizes of regions to convey precise quantitative information.

Some years ago it became fashionable to design maps of the United States in which the sizes of the states were varied, as in "Don't" in Figure 6.8, to show relative rates or quantities—per capita beer consumption, number of murders, and so forth; the more per the state, the larger the area. At best, such maps convey only a rough impression of rank ordering, and fall short if actual amounts or even precise ordering is to be conveyed. We humans simply are not very good at estimating area and have trouble comparing relative areas of differently shaped regions.

- A better way to convey amount is to draw a bar, stacked set of icons, or similar symbols at each location, varying length or height to convey quantity; our visual system can compare relative lengths well.

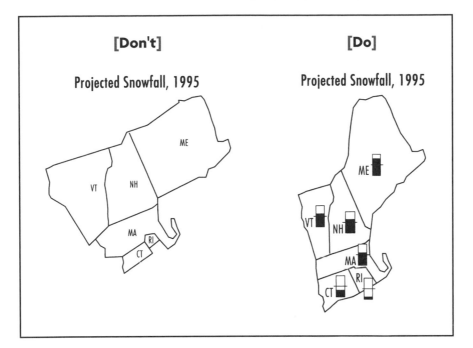

Figure 6.8. It is almost impossible to extract relative amounts from differently shaped areas, even if they are familiar and not distorted. Vary extent along a line or bar instead (the framework around each bar and the short horizontal lines are designed to help viewers compare the black bars).

6. Ensure that shapes of meaningful regions are easily identifiable.

Another problem with varying the size of a region to convey information is that the shape may become unrecognizable. If Maine is made larger, its shape may have to be modified to fit it against its neighbors, as happened in the "Don't" example in Figure 6.8.

7. Don't vary height and width of location markers to specify different types of information.

The map in "Don't" in figure 6.9 uses the height of the markers to indicate the population and the width of the markers to indicate the mean temperature of each location. But our brains register the area of the markers, not each dimension separately. Don't vary a shape's height and width (or—as discussed in Chapter 4—a color's hue, lightness, and saturation) to specify values of distinct dimensions.

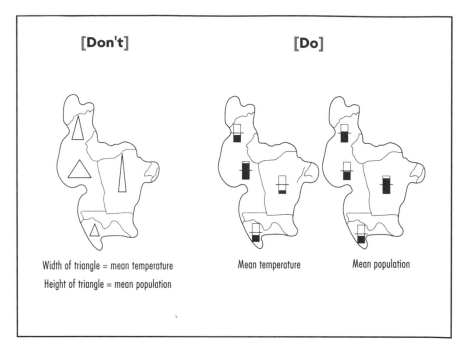

Figure 6.9. If both the width and height of the triangles are varied, we see neither variable very well; it is far better to use two different displays, one for each variable.

8.   Avoid visual illusions that distort distance and direction.

Visual illusions affect our perception of distances. Vertical lines appear longer than horizontal ones, and straight lines that are interrupted, as in "Don't" in Figure 6.10, appear to be displaced; the diagonal road passing under the highway is actually straight, but it appears to jog under the overpass. This is not a problem in "Do".

9.   If distance is important, use grid markings.

Some maps are intended to indicate the relative locations of regions, to show the locations of specific routes, or to provide other kinds of qualitative information. Other maps, however, specify the actual distances between locations. In these cases, inner grids are useful if

- grid lines are relatively thin and light (this recommendation is violated in "Don't" in Figure 6.11).
- more tightly spaced grid lines occur when greater precision is required.
- heavier grid lines are inserted at equal intervals, to help viewers search.
- inner grid lines pass behind the lines, bars, or other symbols.

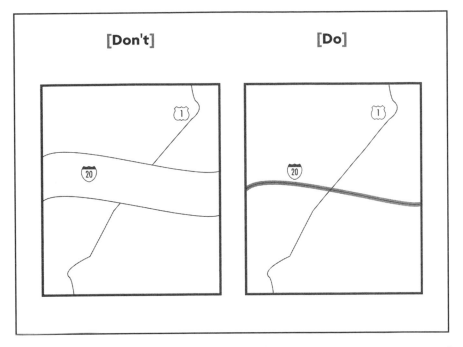

Figure 6.10. Beware of visual illusions (including exaggerated distances of vertical lines) when producing maps. In the map on the left, Route 1 seems to jog as it passes under the Interstate, but in fact it does not.

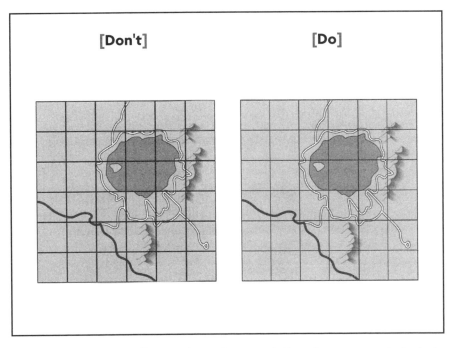

Figure 6.11. If precise distance is not important, there is no reason to include grid lines; if grid lines are included, they should not obscure the features of the territory.

10.   Make the scale equal one or more grid units.

The scale of a map is a kind of key, pairing a line length with a unit of distance, which the viewer uses to estimate the distances between the locations represented on the map. To be effective, the scale should correspond to one or more of the units used to produce the grid lines; if it does not, the viewer will have to reorganize the unit line length, mentally dividing it into the corresponding lengths on the grid—and this operation is neither efficient nor accurate.

- If the grid lines are spaced every half inch on the map, the scale should indicate the distance in terms of this unit length or in terms of a familiar multiple of this increment, say, 1 inch. It's often most useful if the scale indicates a unit that corresponds to the distance between heavy grid lines as in "Do" in Figure 6.12.

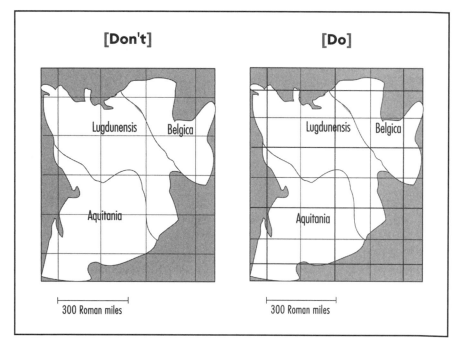

Figure 6.12. If the scale does not line up with the increments of the grids, mental division is necessary to use it; spare the viewer this effort by aligning the scale and grid increments.

11.   Make more important routes more salient.

Use the most important routes as the backbone of the map, as in "Do," in Figure 6.13, allowing other routes to be organized by them. This can be accomplished simply by making the more important routes more visually distinctive, using color or line weight.

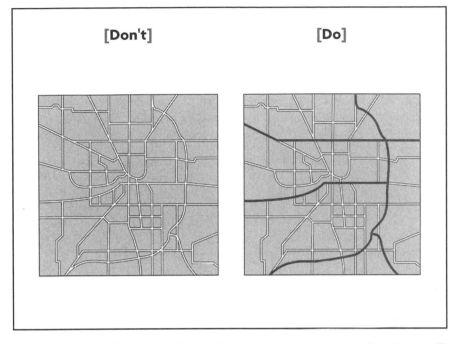

Figure 6.13. Making the major roads correspond to more salient lines will help viewers to organize the map as well as to find the most efficient routes.

12.   Label important distances directly.

If you want the audience to know the distances between specific pairs of locations, draw lines between them and label the distances directly (the lines should indicate routes).

Photographs and Clipart: 10 Recommendations

Photographs and Clipart are perhaps the most insidious types of illustrations, which practically invite abuse. Many of us can't help but succumb to the temptation to include that cute photo, cartoon, or drawing—and we end up distracting the audience and undermining our message. Nevertheless, photos and clipart do have their place.

1.   Use photos and Clipart to define the context.

Clipart can set the stage for your entire presentation or a portion of your presentation, or it can help you make a specific point.

> **Example:** A drawing or cartoon of historical figures, such as Benjamin Franklin, can set the stage for a contemporary treatment of a relevant topic—such as contemporary methods of making bifocal lenses.

2. Use photos and clipart to introduce an abstract idea.

Sometimes very abstract ideas have become associated with concrete icons. Such illustrations can put the audience in a frame of mind to organize what you have to say in terms they already know—which is always a good idea.

> **Example:** Albert Einstein's visage has become a symbol for genius, and the Statue of Liberty has become a symbol of freedom for immigrants.

3. Use photos and Clipart to evoke a specific emotion.

In some situations, you may want your audience to feel a specific emotion. This can be part and parcel of an argument you are making. Research in cognitive neuroscience has shown that many decisions are driven by emotional associations, and thus an important part of any argument is to create the appropriate emotional reactions to points being made.

> **Example:** If you want to argue that additional funds should be allocated for helping the homeless, you might show a series of photos of dispirited and dejected homeless men, women, and children living on the streets of various cities.

4. Use photos to present evidence.

Even in these days of computer graphics, many people still react as if "seeing is believing." Thus, use photos to present evidence for your case. Moreover, presenting both text and a graphic will greatly help your audience retain the information.

> **Example:** If you claim that more people drink tea than coffee worldwide, present a montage of photos of people from different parts of the world drinking tea.

5. Use photos and Clipart to give the audience time to "come up for air".

Photos and Clipart can also be useful as a break in the steady flow of information, allowing the audience a moment to reflect and digest. This is especially the case if the photo or Clipart is humorous.

- If you punctuate your presentation with such graphics, be sure that they are relevant to the ongoing thread of your discussion.
- If they are not, they will derail the viewers and disrupt the line of your argument.

6. Use photos and Clipart to direct the audience's attention.

Because attention is drawn to novel stimuli, if you've been presenting mostly text and then present an illustration, the audience will automatically look at the illustration.

- You can use this to your advantage to introduce a new module of the presentation, or to give the audience "time to come up for air."
- But keep in mind that when their attention is drawn to the illustration, the audience won't read text or listen fully to what you say—so, give them a moment or two to absorb the illustration before going on.

7. Choose photos and Clipart that are representative of your point.

If you use photos or Clipart to illustrate a specific situation, select an illustration of an average, typical example of the type of object or situation.

Example: If you want to discuss the proportion of different sorts of animals that live among humans in urban areas, use an illustration of a pigeon-like bird to illustrate "bird," not a crow or woodpecker.

8. Ensure that the style of photos or Clipart is compatible with your message.

People not only grasp the meaning of photos and Clipart but also register the visual qualities of the illustrations themselves. Ensure that the medium meshes with the message.

Example: Don't use a cute cartoon to illustrate a serious point, and don't use a black-and-white photo to illustrate high-technology.

9.   Ensure that illustrations face the center of the slide.

Objects in illustrations typically have a direction; a face looks to the right or left, a car points in one direction or the other, and so on. The orientation of the object will direct the viewers' attention. If you have a face on the right side of the slide looking off to the right, the viewers will have a tendency to do the same—and thus be looking off-screen, rather than where you want them to be focusing when the next slide appears.

10.   Ensure that photos and Clipart do not become too grainy when inserted into the slide.

Clipart is often drawn from other sources, such as websites (but, again, keep copyright issues in mind when you obtain such downloads). The resolution of the art can vary dramatically, and you should be sure that it does not become grainy if you need to expand the art to make it visible from the rear of the room. Not only does grainy art look bad (and make you look bad by extension), but it also can require effort to understand—never a good idea.

From the Principles to the Point

As usual, these recommendations are based directly the eight psychological principles. I again revisit the principles and note which ones contributed primarily to each of the major recommendations I offer.

Principle of Relevance: Communication is most effective when neither too much nor too little information is presented. (We understand and remember a message more easily when the right amount of detail is used to make the point.)

- Include only graphics that help you make your point.
- Include only the parts of graphics that help you make your point.
- Use a list to convey one relation among several entities.

- Choose a point of view in which all critical aspects of the material are visible.
- Provide neither more nor less detail than required to make the point.

Principle of Appropriate Knowledge: Communication requires prior knowledge of relevant concepts, jargon, and symbols. (We understand and remember a message more easily if it connects to what we already know.)

- Use symbols, concepts, and jargon that are familiar to the audience members.

Principle of Salience: Attention is drawn to large perceptible differences. (Big relative differences grab attention.)

- Use animation and vary salience to guide the audience through the display.
- Explode a diagram to emphasize the shapes or spatial relations of individual parts.
- Make more important routes more salient.
- Use photos and Clipart to direct the audience's attention.

Principle of Discriminability: Two properties must differ by a large enough proportion or they will not be distinguished. (We need contrast to distinguish shapes, colors, or positions from each other and from the background.)

- Ensure that all aspects of the graphic are clearly discriminable from the background.
- Ensure that shapes of meaningful regions are easily identifiable.
- Ensure that photos and clipart do not become too grainy when inserted into the slide.

Principle of Perceptual Organization: People automatically group elements into units, which they then attend to and remember. (These groups are easier to see and remember than the isolated components would be.)

- Organize the components of complex displays.
- Ensure that different components of a diagram are organized into separate perceptual units.
- Use animation to illustrate three-dimensional structure.
- Don't vary height and width of location markers to specify different types of information.
- Don't vary the sizes of regions to convey precise quantitative information.

Principle of Compatibility: A message is easiest to understand if its form is compatible with its meaning. (For better or worse, the mind tends to judge a book by its cover.)

- Use a chart to convey overall organizational structure.
- Use a chart to illustrate sequences of steps over time.
- Show more inclusive categories higher in the display.
- Use a layout compatible with the subject matter.
- Use a diagram to illustrate the structure of an object or event for a specific purpose.
- Use compatible movement when presenting a diagram of a dynamic event.
- Use a map to show distances of segments or angles between segments of a route.
- Use a map if more than one route is possible.
- Avoid visual illusions that distort distance and direction.
- Use photos and Clipart to define the context.
- Use photos and Clipart to introduce an abstract idea.
- Use photos and Clipart to evoke a specific emotion.
- Choose photos and Clipart that are representative of your point.
- Ensure that the style of photos or Clipart is compatible with your message.
- Ensure that illustrations face the center of the slide.

Principle of Informative Changes: People expect changes in properties to carry information. (And we expect every necessary piece of information to be indicated by a change in a perceptible property.)

- Change visual or auditory characteristics only to signal a change in information.
- Identify relationships.
- Show all parts of static diagrams from the same viewpoint.
- Label important distances directly.
- Use a map to label complex sets of information about a territory.

Principle of Capacity Limitations: People have a limited capacity to retain and to process information, and so will not understand a message if too much information must be retained or processed. (From a communicative point of view, less can be more!)

- Respect the *Rule of Four:* Don't expect viewers to attend to more than four perceptual units on a slide.
- Use multiple panels to highlight specific comparisons.
- Don't explode an object too widely for recognition.

- If distance is important, use grid markings.
- Make the scale equal to one or more grid units.
- Use photos to present evidence.
- Use photos and Clipart to give the audience time to "come up for air."

The Good, the Bad, and the Incomprehensible

In this brief chapter we will see the principles in action and then review a daunting set of problems with the PowerPoint program— and these are representative examples. Although all of these problems can be circumvented by someone who is aware of them and knows how to set up slides manually, they nevertheless can lead some presenters astray.

Why am I presenting this material? When teaching, I've discovered that sometimes the best way to explain how to do something correctly is to demonstrate the consequences of doing it badly—in fact, that's why I've often shown "Don't" examples in the preceding pages. I'll begin this final chapter by taking this tack and discussing a single horrendous display in detail. In addition, although I have written this book to be more than instructions on which commands to use and when to use them, I need now to review some potential problems with the PowerPoint program itself so that you can avoid falling prey to them. I identify the problems by considering—you guessed it—the psychological principles. Finally, I will close with a very brief reflection on this medium itself.

The Principles in (In)action

Take a look at Figure 7.1. At one point, federal regulators considered putting such a display on all food packaging in the United States. Try to read this display. Some people are never able to understand it, even if they keep at it; most give up after a first glance. Give yourself a few minutes to try to decipher it before reading the following.

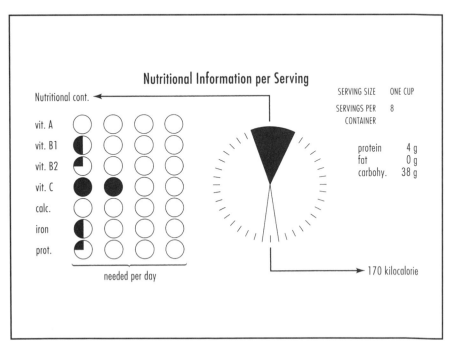

Figure 7.1. A complex display intended to indicate the nutritive content of food. Try to decipher it.

Let's put this dreadful example of information graphics to good use, taking advantage of it to see what happens when the psychological principles are not respected.

The problems are many. In fact, every one of the principles has been violated in this one display!

First, each row of circles in the left panel is meant to indicate the amount of a daily requirement of a vitamin, mineral, or protein. However, the viewer is likely to interpret the small circles as pie graphs (the shape taps into our knowledge of such displays). Pie graphs divide a single whole into its proportions, but each of these circles does not correspond to a single whole. Rather, the total of four circles in each row is supposed to depict a whole. Thus, unless the viewer is familiar with such displays, this device violates the Principle of Appropriate Knowledge.

Furthermore, this arrangement is particularly unfortunate because the circles are positioned closer to the ones above them than to the ones to the sides, and so the grouping law of proximity leads the viewer to see them as organized into columns; in fact, they should be seen as organized into rows. The Principle of Perceptual Organization has been ignored, with the result that the viewers must try to override what they see automatically.

Moreover, the same length row is used in all cases, which violates the Principle of Compatibility; we tend to see more as more, and notice the length of rows before we notice the amount of material in the assembled circles.

Now look at the center panel, which is supposed to convey two different sorts of information: the overall proportion of "Nutritional cont." (actually, vitamins and minerals in the black wedge) and the number of calories (the white wedge) per serving. The Principle of Informative Changes has been violated here; the label is insufficient. Moreover, the Principle of Appropriate Knowledge is again violated because this part of the display uses the technically correct—but less familiar—term "kilocalorie" to mean "calorie."

It is also unfortunate that the wedges line up to form a single shape; the Principle of Perceptual Organization will lead the viewers to think that the two wedges are related, and they are not. In addition, there's a problem in that the panel looks like the familiar pie graph, possibly misleading the viewer into thinking that the two wedges are different proportions of the same whole. And the absence of labels on the arrows forces the viewer to work to figure out that they correspond to different things, "composed of" and "produces" for the left and right arrows, respectively. This is not only a violation of the Principle of Informative Changes but also of the Principle of Capacity Limitations. If the viewer must work to figure out the meaning, the communication is in danger of failing.

But an even more severe violation of the Principle of Capacity Limits is evident: To determine the actual amounts, the viewer must count 40 tick marks around the circle (mentally supplying the missing ones)—a tedious and time-consuming exercise. Also, the tick marks would have been more discriminable if, for example, every 10th mark was bold. Thus, even the Principle of Discriminability has been violated here.

The confusion continues. Notice that protein ("prot.") appears in the leftmost portion of the display and also in the table at the far right; how are these entries related? What is the relation between "170 kilocalorie" and the table at the right about servings? The Principle of Informative Changes has been violated; we need additional marks to help us understand.

And the scattered organization of the table itself makes it hard to read. Moreover, is all of this even relevant to the average consumer? Even without knowing in detail what the average consumer really needs to know, we are led to suspect that the Principle of Relevance has been violated.

Finally, which part of the display is most important? Where should viewers start to read, and how should they proceed through the display? Without using the Principle of Salience appropriately, the viewer is left at sea. And if this display is so daunting in print, think of how much worse it would be on a slide—where the audience has only a limited amount of time to try solve this puzzle.

The problems with displays like this underscore the most fundamental message of this book: To ensure that a display will be clear and to the point, consider the psychological principles summarized in the appendix, both when you design your presentation and then afterward, when you review what you've made. Often it is simply impossible to keep all of the relevant factors in mind while designing a display, and only after you produce a slide can you then check to ensure that you have not accidentally violated the principles.

Examples of Problems with the PowerPoint Program

The PowerPoint program is a useful and versatile tool. But like any other tool, it can be misused. Moreover, some of its features invite misuse. In this section, I review some of the problems. However, keep in mind that depending on your purpose, some of these potential problems may actually work to your advantage. For example, if your goal is to illustrate that an idea is too complicated and unworkable, then a complex graphic may be just the thing. With that in mind, the following are—more often than not, I would hazard—features that invite problems in a presentation.

Design Templates (aka "Themes")

Too many of the design templates offered in the PowerPoint program violate the principles, specifically the Principles of

Salience, by including eye-catching graphics;
Discriminability, by making it difficult to discern text and content, and easy to include too-similar colors for different levels of text;
Perceptual Organization, by including objects that can be grouped too easily with your content;
Informative Changes, by misleading the viewer into thinking there's content where there's only meaningless decoration.

Although the templates are different in various versions of the PowerPoint program, for illustrative purposes it's useful to consider the first three offenders that show up on my version (for the Macintosh)—*Alchemy, Bar Code*, and *Beach*.

Alchemy has a bright splash at the upper left, which draws the viewers' attention to that part of the slide; this is not helpful if text or graphics extend across the full range of the slide. Not only this, but the swirling arcs are distracting and could easily create discriminability problems if content-bearing text or graphics happened to be located over them.

Barcode has an elegant horizontal red slash, which could nicely underline a title. But the red slash stays just where it is, regardless of where the text box is placed. Hence, it can cut right through text. And the bar code pattern beneath it will only obscure text or graphics placed over it.

Beach includes a realistic beach ball and pail, on sand, which are entirely too distracting. Not only are these background elements much too salient, and hence draw attention, but they also would interfere with any other text or graphics. User beware!

On learning that the PowerPoint program for the PC was being revamped for 2007, I was optimistic that practice would make perfect—and that problems like those just noted would be a only a bad memory. But this was not to be. For example:

Apex includes bright rays emanating from the upper left, which not only are too salient, but also make it difficult to discriminate font that is not highly saturated;

Aspect shifts the title from the top to the bottom depending on the layout of the material on the slide, which is distracting at best;

Technic deserves special mention, speaking of odd placement of text, because it puts the subtitle above the title!

The 2007 version also includes specfic design templates, such as *Blue String Strands,* where a bright line is not only far too salient, but can easily cut through text on the title slide and disrupt the ease of reading. But the *Blue Flywheel Design* in the "Business" section is particularly worthy of note: Not only does it picture a large, salient, and meaningless flywheel (at least, I think that's what that thing is), and have rectangular boxes that would cut through many titles or lists, but also the predefined color of the subtitle font is almost indistingusihable from the color of the background! Many of the new templates are actually worse than in the previous version.

Content Templates

Content templates not only provide formats, color schemes, and graphics but also actually provide "suggested text for specific subjects" (I quote from PowerPoint "Help"). For example, there are templates that supposedly help you in a "brainstorming session," to "communicate bad news," and so on. Want to seem insincere? Thoughtless? You run the risk of getting such reactions by using these canned "thoughts" and "ideas."

In addition to including uninspired and uninspiring pointers, some of these templates include bad formatting. For example, in "Employee Orientation" bullet points fly in one-by-one, which can draw attention but also prove a distraction. And in "Selling a Product" (for the Mac), the background "pulses," which is interesting but very distracting (this feature *was* fixed in the "Presentation on Product or Service" template in Office 2007). Furthermore, many templates have default color schemes that reuse the same colors (or very similar colors) to mark different content elements (thereby producing a violation of the Principle of Discriminability).

Other templates (such as "Selling a Product") contain exotic conceptual diagrams, and the user is expected to fill them in (violating the Principles of Appropriate Knowledge, Compatibility, and—often—Informative Changes).

Slide Show Options

Slide show options provide more temptations that should be avoided. For example, the preset text animations include sounds, such as "laser" and "typewriter," which are more likely to distract than orient or inform, and the animation feature "flash once" makes content elements appear and disappear; it isn't clear what purpose this feature could serve in a typical presentation. It usually would violate the Principle of Discriminability.

Chart (and Graph) Options

The following are major problems with the "chart" options in the PowerPoint program. Their term "chart" also includes graphs.

Pie Charts

The PowerPoint program prevents you from modifying "pie charts" (i.e., pie graphs) in several ways that would improve them. For example, in the Mac version you cannot explode one, and only one, wedge. It's either all or nothing, which violates both the Principles of Informative Changes and Discriminability. It also does not place wedge labels inside the pie, which violates the Principle of Perceptual Organization. (Both of these problems have thankfully been fixed in Office 2007 for the PC.)

In addition, the program has options and default settings that get in the way of making effective pie graphs. For example, when making black-and-white pie graphs, dot spacing is used to distinguish the parts rather than hatching or different gray-scale values; this practice violates the Principle of Discriminability. Office 2007 does use different gray scales, but they are not necessarily discriminable.

The PowerPoint program also allows the unwary user to create a "donut" where the center of a pie is removed—this violates the Principle of Appropriate Knowledge and could confuse more than illuminate. The Program also can create a "pie of pie" and a "bar of pie" in which some of the values are extracted from the original pie and put into a new pie or bar connected by lines to the old one. Because the "whole" is split across two displays, this can easily be misleading and confusing. What audience could immediately grasp such displays?

Line Charts

Next, consider "Line Charts" (i.e., line graphs) and scatterplots. The default in the PowerPoint program does not label lines directly (but instead uses a key), which forces you to do so by hand or to use the key (which would thereby force the viewer to memorize the key and then search for the corresponding lines). The program also does not by default indicate a discontinuity in a scale via slash marks or a zigzag, which may thereby violate the Principle of Compatibility (because more may not look like more). And it also doesn't indicate when points overlap in a scatterplot; one is simply hidden by the other, which is a violation of both the Principles of Informative Changes and Compatibility. In addition, many of the default settings in the PowerPoint program are not optimal. For example, axis category labels are made bold but the axis value labels are not, which violates the Principle of Informative Changes, and the weight of the line illustrating the content line is 2 point, whereas the weight of the lines for the axes is less than 1 point. This makes the axes less salient than they should be.

The PowerPoint program also has the reverse problem: When it does provide options, some of them invite the user to make less-than-optimal displays. For example, the program can display the written coordinates next to every data point, which creates clutter and taxes our limited processing capacity. It also can display a table below a graph, which introduces unnecessary redundancy—and can confuse the viewers if they expect every visual change to reflect new information (Principle of Informative Changes). In addition, in the 2007 version for the PC, you can present only the lines from a line graph—with no axes, no gridlines, and no labels of any kind. It is difficult to imagine a circumstance in which the audience would find such an uninformative display informative.

Moreover, the PowerPoint program can also connect the points in a scatterplot with lines, creating an almost menacing, confusing spider web (without conveying any useful information in the process).

Bar Charts

"Bar Charts" (i.e., bar graphs) not only have the same problems with axes and labeling that exist for line graphs but have additional ones as well. For example, they can display one variable as bars and the other variable as area, such that the amount of shaded area is relevant to one variable but not the other. This violates not only the Principle of Appropriate Knowledge but also the Principle of Capacity Limitations (forcing people to work hard to compare the two types of variables). In addition, it can substitute cones for bars (included cones with colors to indicate different layers within them), which makes it difficult to tell what values are being depicted.

The PowerPoint program also can show more than one row of three-dimensional bars on the same graph such that one row hides the other—thereby not signaling information with visible changes. You can avoid this option, but the fact that presenters can easily stumble into using it is unfortunate.

Three-Dimensional Displays

The addition of the third dimension to a graph is a mixed blessing. For many purposes, it does no harm and makes the presentation more interesting (see the literature review in my book, *Graph Design for the Eye and Mind*). However, for other purposes it disrupts communication by obscuring the precise amounts displayed (such as occurs when the tops of bars are not clearly aligned with values on a wall that serves as the Y axis). With such concerns in mind, it is worth approaching with caution the following characteristics of the program's three-dimensional displays:

- They can change the elevation of one's vantage point from the 15-degree default to less than 90 degrees (a view from below) to more than 90 degrees (a view from above). A view from above will not show relative heights, and thereby obscures differences in amounts being shown.
- The program allows you to rotate the graph in any direction, which can completely obscure differences between bars and lines.
- Because of the angle at which the axes meet, the ratio of the X axis to the Y axis can produce misleading patterns.

Organizational Chart Options

Finally, let's consider another type of display, the organizational chart (included in the Smart Art Graphics in Office 2007). The PowerPoint program can designate one of six (or seven, depending on the version of the program) styles to represent groups of coworkers, which potentially violates the Principle of Appropriate Knowledge. Styles that attempt to balance the number of coworkers placed on each side of a vertical line have inherently confusing hierarchical relations. Moreover, levels in a hierarchy, which can be selected individually, don't necessarily correspond to tiers of the chart (thereby violating the Principle of Compatibility). In an apparent step backward, Office 2007 for the PC allows hierarchical relations to be presented using 3D graphics, which invites the problems noted above.

Don't Shoot the Messenger

Do these problems imply that giving PowerPoint presentations is a bad idea, that we should abandon it and return to the older methods of communicating? Tufte, in his essay "The Cognitive Style of PowerPoint," answers this question with a resounding "Yes." Tufte decries what is lost when the PowerPoint program leads people to create bulleted lists and low-resolution graphics. He looks back fondly to an era when slides could be held in the hand and physically inserted into a projector, when slides had very high resolution so people could present huge data tables, when making slides was sufficiently difficult that people often substituted the spoken word for the visible list—and thereby, he implies, audiences were treated to more eloquent and cogent discourse than is typically found in today's lecture halls.

When I was reading Tufte's essay, a vision came unbidden to my mind: I visualized two orators in ancient Mesopotamia, one rushing to tell the other about the invention of this new system called "writing." He said, with a note of anxiety in his voice, "Zuqiqïpum, you won't believe this. They make wedges in clay and use them to freeze words. They squeeze the emotion out of our living language. They remove the creativity, the warmth, the very humanity from the words! What a desecration!!" I imagined that in the years that followed, every time these two gentlemen read a bad poem or story, they blamed not the author but rather the existence of writing itself.

But, of course, the existence of writing is not itself responsible for bad poems and bad stories any more than it is responsible for good poems and good stories. The medium does not determine the message; ultimately, the responsibility for a bad poem, story, or essay (or presentation) rests not on the medium but on the person using it. Moreover, nobody was telling the orators to stop doing what they did best, which was to enrapture audiences with their performances. Rather, the technology of writing had opened new doors, inviting new ways to keep precise records and allowing many more people to enjoy aspects of culture that previously had been limited to the privileged few.

Each new communication technology does not *replace* previous technologies. The computer has not replaced calligraphy any more than the mass publication of sheet music replaced the live performance of string quartets. Each new technology adds options to what was there before—and these options can be put to good use or to bad use. This book provides advice about how best to use the newest link in this long, long chain.

For many purposes, PowerPoint presentations are a superior medium of communication, which is why they have become standard in so many fields. This medium affords a world of possibilities and is an extraordinarily powerful tool. I hope that the recommendations in this book can help you to exploit the strengths of the PowerPoint program without being tripped up by its weaknesses. If I've been successful, you should now not only be familiar with a slew of recommendations, but you should also have developed intuitions about how presentations can be designed to mesh well with the nature of human mental processes. The recommendations and intuitions will help you make your presentations clear and to the point—and will lead you on the path to becoming a true PowerPoint Jedi, not a PowerPoint Sith. Embrace the future, avoid the dark side, and harness the power of your creativity!

Appendix: Psychological Principles and Their Specific Aspects

In this appendix I summarize the 8 principles in more detail, providing enough information for you to use them as guidance in situations not discussed in the previous pages.

Relevance

The Principle of Relevance: Communication is most effective when neither too much nor too little information is presented.

People unconsciously try to organize information into concepts or narratives. It's almost as if we have an "urge to understand" or an "urge to explain." If you don't provide enough information to make your case, the audience will be left with fragments of the story and will flail about, trying to fill in the missing pieces (assuming that they are motivated; if not, they will probably give up and tune you out). Less obvious, because we try to fit related material into a single concept or narrative, you can also confuse by presenting too much information. Again, the audience will try to fit all of the pieces together, and additional details will require additional effort. The audience needs to know what's the foreground and what's the background—what's important and what's context. If you present too much, the audience may have trouble making this distinction. So, before beginning to prepare your presentation, you need to decide what message you want to convey; only after you have made this decision can you determine what information to include.

Appropriate Knowledge

The Principle of Appropriate Knowledge: Communication requires prior knowledge of pertinent concepts, jargon, and symbols.

After you have decided *what* to say, you need to determine *how* to say it. You will communicate effectively only if you make use of what the audience members already know. Ideally, rely only on concepts, jargon, and symbols that are familiar to your audience; if novel concepts, jargon, or symbols must be used, define them. But more than that, respect the fact that we humans understand new information by relating it to information previously stored in memory. To understand these words, for instance, you need to have stored their meanings previously. As a general rule, the audience will understand a new idea most easily if it is presented as growing out of a familiar one. For instance, if you are presenting a plan to market air conditioners in rural China to an audience that is very familiar with marketing products in international markets, you might draw an analogy to how a previous market was opened (perhaps rural Australia)—or how a similar product (perhaps electric heaters) broke into the same market.

Salience

The Principle of Salience: Attention is drawn to large perceptible differences.

We are led to focus first on the most prominent features of a display, those that are brighter, darker, larger, in motion, or in some other way clearly different from their surroundings. This ability is very important, both for our current survival and that of our ancestors. Thus, it's no surprise that an ancient part of the brain, the superior colliculus (for vision), produces a kind of "attentional reflex." This part of the brain is functional almost immediately after birth, whereas the parts of the brain required to shift attention voluntarily become functional only a month or two after birth. As a consequence of the relative ages when the two sorts of mechanisms come "online," young babies are subject to "attentional capture": A flashing light might grab their attention, and then they are stuck looking at that glittering object until something else grabs their attention. The same is true for sound: We reflexively pay attention to louder or different-pitched sounds.

The key to salience is not the absolute properties of a sight or sound, but its properties in comparison to those of the background or other elements. When you read **THIS** the word "this" is salient; BUT WHEN YOU READ THIS THE WORD "THIS" IS NOT.

Discriminability

The Principle of Discriminability: Two properties must differ by a large enough proportion or they will not be distinguished.

This principle derives from basic characteristics of how neurons (i.e., brain cells) interact. Consider neurons that detect spots of light in the first portions of the cerebral cortex to receive input from the eyes. Nearby neurons tend to inhibit each other: If one is strongly activated, it tries to "turn off" its neighbors. This arrangement apparently plays a role in specifying the locations of edges, say, between a piece of white paper and the unpainted wooden table top on which it rests. The inhibition allows the system to sharpen up the boundary between the two regions (paper and table top), because the neurons that are stimulated more by the light bouncing off the paper will inhibit those on the other side of the edge. However, if the paper were on a white table top, it would be much more difficult to see it, its edges would not be so well defined. Similar effects occur for all sensory inputs; we register differences more easily when there are larger disparities in values. In general, a constant proportion of the smaller property's value must be added in order for a larger value to be distinguishable (this is known as Weber's law).

This principle applies to size, lightness, thickness, density of dots, cross-hatching, and types of dashes. A special case of discriminability occurs when marks must be large enough or different enough in color or weight to be discriminated from the background, and hence be noticed—and if they aren't noticed, they may as well not exist.

Perceptual Organization

The Principle of Perceptual Organization: People automatically group elements into units, which they then attend to and remember.

The world is not like the diagram of a cow on a butcher's wall: There are no dotted lines that specify how to organize it. Rather, our brains must produce this organization. So important is this task that numerous different mechanisms have evolved to accomplish it. In the text, I focused on just the grouping laws but sometimes had to refer to other aspects of the principles that underlie the way we organize visual input. I here summarize all of the relevant principles.

Grouping Laws

The visual system automatically groups perceptible elements into perceptual units. Because a unit is a psychological—not a physical— entity, we cannot determine whether a slide has too much information simply by counting marks on the screen. Rather, we must understand how perceptual organization works.

Proximity

People group together nearby marks. For example, you see "xxx xxx" as two groups, whereas you will see the same number of elements presented as "xx xx xx" as three groups. Thus, for instance, putting labels in tables closer to the rows and columns that they label than to anything else will automatically group them with the proper column. Similarly, pausing in the middle of a sentence separates words in time, which leads listeners to organize them into separate groups.

Similarity

People group similar marks. For example, you see " - - - -llll " as two groups, and " --ll--ll " as four groups (or, as two groups with two groups within each). This method of grouping plays an especially important role when different colors are used in a display; by matching the colors of items and their labels, the two will automatically be grouped together.

Good continuation

People see segments that line up on a smooth curve as a single unit. For example, you see "- - - - - - - -" as one unit, not eight separate dashes. In contrast, you see "- - - - ‿ ‿ ‿ ‿" as two units, because the dashes now line up as two smooth functions.

Common fate

People group together marks that are moving similarly. For instance, if you have material glide in from one side of a slide, viewers will group parts of the same word or figure that move at the same rate and at the same time.

Good form

People group marks that form simple shapes, such as "[_]," which we see as one shape; in contrast when the same marks are arranged so that they do not form a simple shape, "] [_ ," we see them individually.

Input channels

What we see comes to us from a number of "input channels," which you can think of as analogous to different lenses on a camera (they focus on smaller or larger regions, with higher or lower resolution, respectively). These channels differ partly in regard to the size of the region they register, which also affects the amount of detail they pick up. Less detail is detected when larger regions are monitored. For instance, when seen from 10 feet away, one channel might register objects as large as a car, but not much detail; another might register objects as large as a motorcycle, but with more detail; another, objects as large as a TV set, with even more detail; and finally, another might register objects as large as a cell phone, in great detail. Which channel is "best"? That depends on the task at hand. For walking around a car, output from a channel that picks up large shapes would be most helpful; for threading a needle, output from a channel that registers fine detail would be most helpful.

The acuity (level of detail) of a channel is described by its "spatial frequency," which is the number of regular light/dark changes (for example, light and dark stripes of equal width) that fit into a specific amount of your visual field. Each channel responds to a range of light-dark alternations (such as dashes in a line, or stripes in a pattern) of roughly 2 to 1. Thus, when we look at an area of evenly spaced hatch lines, dots, or patches, we will also mentally take in, like it or not, areas of other similarly oriented lines, dots, or patches whose light-dark cycles range from half as frequent to twice as frequent. The closer the spacing is to the spacing in the area we are supposed to pay attention to, the harder it is to ignore.

Therefore, viewers will immediately see that two evenly spaced hatch lines, dots, or patches are separate if they differ by more than a ratio of 2 to 1 (e.g., if one line has 4 dashes to the inch, viewers will immediately see as different any other line that does not fall in the range between 2 and 8 dashes to the inch).

The visual system also has channels that are sensitive to different orientations. Studies of discrimination of lines at different orientations have shown that when lines differ by at least 30 degrees (the angle formed by the hands of a clock when they point to adjacent numbers, as at 12:05), we can distinguish among them without having to pay close attention. Viewers will immediately see that differently oriented hatch marks (e.g., parallel lines used to distinguish regions) are distinct if the lines are rotated at least 30 degrees apart.

Integrated versus separated dimensions

We perceive combinations of visual properties in two distinct ways. On the one hand, properties along *separable dimensions* can be registered individually; a viewer can pay attention to one variable and ignore the other. For instance, the color and length of a line are separable, as are the length and orientation of a line. On the other hand, an element's *integral dimensions* can be seen individually only with difficulty; these properties are automatically combined by the visual system. In particular, we cannot pay attention to the height of a shape without also registering the width and the resulting area, and cannot pay attention to hue without also registering saturation and lightness. This is why different information should not be conveyed by the height and width of a shape or by hue and saturation or lightness.

Spatial imprecision

Different neural pathways register shapes and spatial relations, and the outputs from these pathways are not always combined properly or precisely. We register precise spatial relations (e.g., between parts of an exploded diagram) only with effort. External aids, such as grid lines in a graph, can help the viewer apprehend spatial relations among shapes precisely.

The various aspects of the Principle of Perceptual Organization are summarized in Table 1.

Table 1. Aspects of the Principle of Perceptual Organization

Aspect	Specific Cases	Explanation	Example
Grouping Laws	Proximity	Nearby marks are grouped together	XXXX vs. XX XX
	Similarity	Similar marks are grouped together	OOXX vs. OXOX
	Good continuation	Marks along a smooth function are grouped together	-------- vs. ---- ----
	Common fate	Marks moving the same way are grouped together	→ . . vs. ← . . →
	Good form	Marks that define a simple figure are grouped together	( ) vs. (__
Input Channels	Acuity	Marks that vary in frequency by less than a 2-1 ratio will be seen together	- - - - - - - -------- versus -------- __ ___ ___
	Orientation	Lines that vary in orientation by less than 30 degrees will be seen together	The hour hand of a clock at 1:00 versus at 1:30
Integrated versus Separated Dimensions	Separable	Dimensions that are seen independently	The size of a circle and the orientation of a radius within it
	Integral	Dimensions that are not seen independently	The height and width of a rectangle
Spatial Imprecision		We do not always precisely organize objects in terms of their spatial relations	The relation between a line in a graph and a point on the Y axis is not easy to see precisely

Compatibility

The Principle of Compatibility: A message is easiest to understand if its form is compatible with its meaning.

This principle also has several distinct aspects, as follows.

Appearance-Meaning Correspondence

What you see should be what you get. The Stroop phenomenon (discussed in Chapter 1, where people have difficulty naming the color of ink used to print words that name colors when the ink color is different from the color name) is an extreme example of what goes wrong when this principle is violated.

More Is More

Greater amounts along a visual dimension are interpreted as representing larger amounts of a measured substance or quality. For instance, larger wedges in a pie are seen as representing greater amounts, as are higher bars or higher points on a line.

Cultural Conventions

All cultures produce common associations between some visual characteristics and concepts. For example, in Western culture, increases commonly are indicated from left to right or in a direction clockwise around a circle. But these associations are not shared worldwide, and the conventions of your audience should not be contravened (e.g., during the height of the Cultural Revolution in China, some firebrands wanted to reverse the meaning of red and green in stoplights, making red mean "go").

Perceptual Distortion

The eye and mind are sometimes prone to distort the actual physical form we perceive and may distort in systematic ways. Thus, compatibility must be considered not simply in terms of the physical characteristics of an object or event, but instead in terms of how those characteristics are perceived. Some visual dimensions are systematically distorted, most important:

- We progressively underestimate area as the amount of area increases.
- Although we register line length relatively accurately, vertical lines appear longer than horizontal ones of the same length. Hence, it is difficult to compare vertical with horizontal or vice versa.
- Another source of distortion arises from our tendency to see patterns as reflecting three-dimensional objects. People have difficulty comparing the sizes of, or spatial relations among, objects that are pictured at different distances.

The aspects of the Principle of Compatibility are summarized in Table 2.

Table 2. Aspects of the Principle of Compatibility

Aspect	Explanation	Example
Appearance-Meaning Correspondence	The interpretation of a pattern should not conflict with its meaning	A penguin should not be used to represent birds in general
More Is More	Greater quantities should be represented by greater perceptible properties	Higher or longer bars should represent greater quantities
Cultural Conventions	The interpretation of a pattern should be consistent with its cultural interpretation	Figures on the left should not represent conservatives in the U.S., nor should figures on the right represent liberals
Perceptual Distortion	We don't always accurately register what we see or hear	Area is underestimated; vertical lines appear longer than horizontal ones

Informative Changes

The Principle of Informative Changes: People expect changes in properties to carry information.

When things stay the same, there is no new information; when something changes, there is — or should be — new information. If a noticeable change in the appearance or the sound of your presentation doesn't mean something, the change is simply a distraction. In addition, every piece of necessary information should be signaled by a perceptible change — visible marks or audible sounds. Suitable links and labels should be shown, as should signs indicating that a different sort of information (e.g., projections of future trends, or different types of measurements) is being presented.

Finally, when the same word or illustration conveys more than one meaning it is, by definition, ambiguous. The audience should not have to struggle to resolve ambiguity, in either words or graphics, but rather should be provided the information as directly and transparently as possible. You can specify the appropriate meaning of an ambiguous word either by paraphrasing it or providing the appropriate context (e.g., the word "port" is not ambiguous in the context of boats or wines). Ambiguity in graphics can be eliminated either by presenting concrete, specific examples or by providing clear labels (which may be a phrase if an individual word would be ambiguous).

Capacity Limitations

The Principle of Capacity Limitations: People have a limited capacity to retain and to process information, and so will not understand a message if too much information must be retained or processed.
    This principle has two parts, Memory Limitations and Processing Limitations.

Memory Limitations

To follow a presentation, the audience must not only keep in mind what they are seeing and hearing at each moment but also must recall earlier material in order to integrate each new piece into the emerging overall picture. These requirements present a challenge to the speaker because both our ability to hold information in mind and to store information in our memories is limited. However, you can work surprisingly well within these limitations if you organize and present your material properly.

Short-term Memory Limitations
To hold information in mind, we rely on *short-term memory*. We humans can hold in mind (i.e., retain in short-term memory) only about four groups of information at the same time. These groups are technically known as *chunks*, and the process of forming these groups is known as *chunking*. I refer to this as the Rule of Four.

Hierarchical Organization
More fundamentally, here's a crucial point about short-term memory that can be exploited generally: Although we can only hold about four units in mind at once, each of those units itself can include four units. Thus, organizing material hierarchically can vastly improve the ability to hold information in mind.

Privileges of the First and Last
Another aspect of memory that is important for presentations is that we tend to remember best material at the beginning and ending of a sequence. For instance, if I asked you to remember a list of countries where a specific business opportunity is likely to arise in the

near future, such as Japan, France, Pakistan, Norway, Italy, China, Egypt, Mexico, Peru, and Singapore, you would tend to remember the countries at the beginning of the list (such as Japan and France) and those at end of the list (such as Egypt, Peru, and Singapore). We hold the last four or so items in short-term memory, but must store the first few items in *long-term memory,* the relatively permanent store where information is retained even when we are not consciously aware of knowing it. Because short-term memory is too limited to hold all the items at once, we need to store the initial items in long-term memory. And because we have more time to think about ("process") the items we get earlier in the sequence, they are more likely to have been stored than the items in the middle of the sequence. Thus, the middle items are especially vulnerable to being forgotten; they are not in short-term memory and the person hasn't processed them enough to store them in long-term memory.

The bottom line: Put the most important material at the beginning or end of a section (which is one reason I recommend summarizing at the ends of sections).

Hanging it on Memory's Hooks

Part of the reason we recall the first and last best is that we are limited in how well we store information in long-term memory. A good presentation can maximize the probability that information will be retained. One way to improve the audience's memory is to show how new material relates to information the audience members have already stored. We recall variations on a theme better than entirely new information, as I noted earlier.

Thinking Is Learning

An extraordinarily effective way to help your audience learn your material is to lead them to think about it. The more people think through facts or ideas, the more likely they are later to remember this material. For example, in one study, people were asked to visualize scenes described by sentences and simply to rate how vivid each mental image was—with no warning that they would be asked to recall the sentences. When these people later received a surprise memory test, they did just as well as another group who were told from the outset that they should try to memorize the sentences. The more someone is led to "work through" an idea, the more likely he or she is to store it in long-term memory—and hence to be able to remember it much later.

Multiple Memories

Finally, there is more than one type of long-term memory, and retention is vastly improved if people are led to store information in more than one type of memory. In particular, people store words and the appearance of objects in separate memory stores. As I've noted earlier, this means that if you show your audience a picture of an object and name that picture, they will have at least two shots at remembering it—via a memory of how you named it and via a memory of how it actually looked. Showing and telling are better than either showing or telling alone.

Processing Limitations

Humans have only a limited ability to process information.

Effortful Search

Searching a display requires effort, and if too much effort is required the viewer will give up. So vary salience in order to guide the viewer through a display.

Tiring Transformations

Asking the audience to add, subtract, or average values is a sure way to lose them. People do not like to expend effort, especially if they are not sure what the payoff will be.

The various aspects of the Principle of Capacity Limitations are summarized in Table 3.

Table 3. Aspects of the Principle of Capacity Limitations

Aspect	Specific Cases	Explanation	Example
Memory Limitations	Short-term memory limitations	We can hold only 4 groups of information in mind at the same time	We can keep in mind 4 entries in a list
	Chunking	Individual items can be organized into units, each of which can contain up to 4 units and still be held in short-term memory	Hierarchical organization
	Privileges of the First and Last	The first and last entries in a sequence are remembered better than entries in the middle	The beginning and end of a presentation are remembered better than the body of the presentation
	Hanging It on Memory's Hooks	Information is learned more easily if it is a variation of familiar information	Use analogies as such "hooks" in memory to explain a new idea

Continued

Table 3. Continued

Aspect	Specific Cases	Explanation	Example
	Thinking Is Learning	The more people think through material, the more likely they are to remember it	Asking the audience to answer a question will force them to think about it
	Multiple Memories	Multiple copies of memories can be created in different modalities (such as verbal vs. visual)	Using words and pictures increases memory compared to using either one alone
Processing Limitations	Effortful Search	Searching for sought information requires effort	Searching for corresponding labels in multiple panels
	Tiring Transformations	Adding, subtracting, or otherwise transforming information requires effort	Asking viewers to find mean values from entries in a table

Index